A Gardener's Guide to
FROST

A Gardener's Guide to
FROST

OUTWIT THE WEATHER AND EXTEND THE SPRING AND FALL SEASONS

by Philip Harnden

Willow Creek® PRESS

MINOCQUA, WISCONSIN

Table of Contents

Acknowledgments

No one gardens alone. We all benefit from the advice and generosity of other gardeners. In my case, I am especially indebted to the teachers of the North Country Garden School, who so generously shared their knowledge of cold-climate gardening in our workshops and at other events. They include Don Butters, Mary-Ann Cateforis, Ron Dunning, Doug Egeland, Richard Grover, Valarie Hallett, Becky Harblin, Doug Jones, Dick and Joan Kepes, Anneke Larrance, Bill and Di MacKentley, Sandy Maine, Irma and Norbert Markert, Pat Nelson, Don O'Shea, Ellen Rocco, Susan Schwartz, David Sipher, John Sipos, Steve VanderMark, Peter Van de Water, and Steve Wilson. For traveling from afar to give presentations for North Country Garden School, I wish to thank Eliot Coleman, Barbara Damrosch, Jane Kuitems, Paul Longacre, Roger Swain, and Don Ziegler.

I have been blessed with good neighbors who are also good gardeners. I am particularly grateful for what I've learned from Nancy and Todd Alessi, Gary Berk, Leo Burger, Spindle Corey, Denise Dingman, Carolyn Filippi, Elia Filippi, Bonnie Gardinier, Gale Hannan, John McCloskey, Thelma Meites, Isis Melhado, Ellen Rocco, Eleanor Rosenthal, Lisa Thomas, Bryan Thompson, and Jennifer Vincent-Barwood. And my time in the garden would not have been nearly so delightful without the constant companionship (and occasional mole control) of Scratch and Brownie.

For their special input and encouragement on this book, I owe a debt of gratitude to Leo Burger, John Green, and Rodney Houser. To managing editor Andrea Donner and all those who labor behind the scenes at Willow Creek Press, I give my thanks for their expert, guiding hands and for their thoughtfulness.

And lastly, I give my thanks and my heart to M. J. Heisey: twenty-five springs and twenty-five summers, still my favorite gardener.

Roger B. Swain Foreword

Frost provides the punctuation in a northern garden. Here in New Hampshire, we were picking grapes in our shirtsleeves just a week ago, sweating in the hot afternoon sun. This morning the lawn is a crisp white sheet, a skim of ice tops the rain barrel, and the green tomatoes left in the garden are rock hard. When the first frost falls as it has this year, on a clear, half-moon night with the temperature plunging to 24 degrees, there is no mistaking its significance. It signals full stop. Period.

Frost isn't always this definite. There are frosts that blacken my neighbor Pete's garden, located half a mile down the hill, that leave mine untouched, and frosts that settle so lightly that they leave only the tiniest scorch on cucumber foliage after the sun has risen.

Talk of frost is a part of nearly every conversation we have with our neighbors after Labor Day. We take icy thoughts to bed and get up in the middle of the night to check the thermometer, to go outside and feel the grass to see if the dew has fallen. To cover or not to cover, that is the real question. And second-guessers get to stand naked among the tomatoes at midnight draping them by flashlight, an instance of cold-blooded survival at the expense of the warm.

When the much-anticipated frost does finally arrive, we record the date for posterity. And we scan the mosaic of white that morning, looking for untouched places, spots where the sensitive fern still lives, where the grass blades are still wet, signs of warm pockets where tender plants might next year find a few more weeks of safety. But when all has been said, done, and recorded, we know that every growing season must come to an end and that here in the north endings are properly punctuated by ice.

There are places in this country where this isn't true, where the climate offers gardeners no rest, where the growing season is one, long, run-on sentence. With nothing to stop, or even slow, vegetation's advance, the most wielded tool is, I've been told by a San Diego gardener, a good sharp pair of pruning shears. I can't imagine what it must be like to live in such torrid climate. Surely gardeners in such regions must feel a bit like exhausted lion tamers, spinning in center ring as they address their plants in an endless attempt to keep them safely in their places.

Those of us who live in the northern climates belong to a different union. "There is a fraternity of the cold, to which I am glad I belong," E. B. White wrote from his saltwater farm in North Brooklyn, Maine. White, best known for *Charlotte's Web* and other childhood classics, listed his occupation as "Farmer, other." Farming offered White almost unlimited opportunities to put off writing. "Today I should carry the pumpkins and squash from the back porch to the attic. The nights are too frosty to leave them outdoors any longer," began a piece called "Memorandum," a lexicon of little chores he planned to do first on a fall day in 1941.

Among writers, White is best remembered not for what he wrote but for how he wrote it, for the crispness of his prose, and above all for his re-publication of *The Elements of Style,* a slender guide to English usage written by William Strunk, Jr., one of White's professors when he was a student at Cornell.

It seems appropriate that White, with his northern agricultural perspective, should have become punctuation's champion. "Vigorous writing is concise," insisted William Strunk, Jr. Those of us who garden in places where there are only a hundred or so frost-free days perforce do so concisely. We know well that tender plants have a finite life span and that sentences and seasons, no matter how we may choose to lengthen them, must both come to an end. Period.

Yet, as the following pages deftly illustrate, a life with frost can be lived well indeed. "Get the little book!" commanded E. B. White at the end of his own introduction. Most writers already have. Anyone who gardens between the ice crystals will need this instructive volume as well.

—Roger B. Swain

Gardening with Frost

"What a beautiful summer we had," a northern gardener once told a friend from down south. "I just wish it had been on a weekend so we *all* could have enjoyed it."

Where I garden—in northern New York State along the Canadian border—our summers often seem about that short. I often have frost in my garden, sometimes even in July or August.

Your garden may not be that frigid, but chances are, it's troubled by frost at times. After all, only 25 percent of the earth's entire continental area is absolutely out of the reach of frost—so we have lots of company.

Over the years, I've been fortunate enough to meet many gardeners in my area who aren't intimidated by our short, cool gardening season. They've taught me a lot about how to garden with Jack Frost looking over my shoulder. Or perhaps I should say they've taught me how to garden while looking over my shoulder for Jack Frost.

I've gathered many of those ideas into this book. Together you and I are going to explore all about frost—how to see it coming, how to get ready for it, and how to fend it off. You'll learn to look at your own garden the way Jack Frost does, so you'll understand how to keep it thriving despite those icy visits. You'll even meet some gardeners who have devised ways to keep on gardening right past fall frosts and into winter.

I should tell you right at the beginning that the focus of this book is on the *kitchen garden*—the garden I know best. And we'll mostly concern ourselves with *vegetables*, not fruits, and *annuals*, not perennials. Even so, you can apply most of the ideas in this book to whatever garden you grow and wherever you grow it.

By the end, I hope you'll agree that we gardeners needn't have a siege mentality toward frost. It's not a villain, holding us hostage in some pitifully short gardening season. Jack Frost is simply one more character in this dazzling, sometimes perplexing, and wonderfully rewarding practice we call gardening.

We can learn to garden *with* frost.

Chapter 1

Getting Acquainted with Your Climate

All gardening begins with a question. Before you order your seeds, before you lay out your rows, before you turn over that first spadeful of fragrant spring soil, you must answer this question. In fact, anyone who hopes to succeed as a gardener must first answer it.

The question is: Where am I?

Most of what you do in your garden will be determined by your answer to that simple question. Actually, it's not so simple a question. To answer it, you'll have to do several things.

First, you'll need to look down toward your feet, at the soil. To have a successful garden, you need to know something about your soil's condition. Is it clay? sand? loam?

Is it rich in nutrients or deficient in some? What is its pH: acid, alkaline, or somewhere in the middle? And what about the soil structure? Is it compacted? Or does it contain enough decomposing plant matter to give it the tilth, the light and airy structure, of a good growing medium? The answers to these questions will determine to some extent which vegetables you can easily grow—and which will require extra work on your part.

Next, you'll need to look up toward the sky—that is, you'll have to learn about the precipitation in your garden. How much rain do you get? Enough to grow the crops you want to grow? Or will you need some sort of auxiliary watering system? Or, better yet, what crops are suited to this amount of rainfall?

As you reflect on all this, you may also begin to ponder some related questions. Who gardened here before you? What did they grow here? What can you learn from them? Who will garden here after you? What can your garden teach them? These are questions that fascinate gardeners for their whole lives.

So, you see, you can answer that fundamental gardening question—Where am I?—in several ways. You can answer it in terms of soil conditions or precipitation, or even in terms of history. But now let's ask the question again, thinking this time about *frost*.

Where am I? To answer in terms of frost, you will have to get acquainted with your climate and its weather. Remember that *weather* refers to atmospheric conditions and events: heat and cold, wetness and dryness, calm or storm, and so forth. *Climate* refers to the atmospheric conditions and events that usually prevail in a particular region. Climate is weather in a particular place. Now, to fully know where you are—where you garden— you must be acquainted with your climate.

Climate Zones

Gardeners have several ways of talking about climate. For example, we sometimes speak of *climate zones*. I might ask a gardener in another part of North America, What zone are you in? Usually, I'm referring to the zones designated on the United States

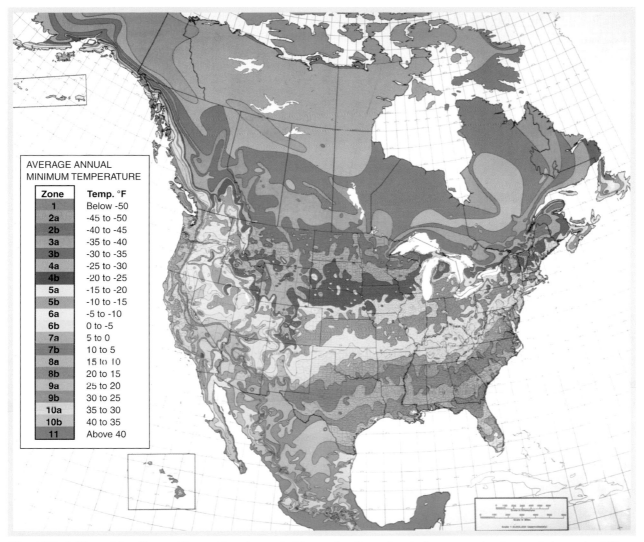

AVERAGE ANNUAL MINIMUM TEMPERATURE

Zone	Temp. °F
1	Below -50
2a	-45 to -50
2b	-40 to -45
3a	-35 to -40
3b	-30 to -35
4a	-25 to -30
4b	-20 to -25
5a	-15 to -20
5b	-10 to -15
6a	-5 to -10
6b	0 to -5
7a	5 to 0
7b	10 to 5
8a	15 to 10
8b	20 to 15
9a	25 to 20
9b	30 to 25
10a	35 to 30
10b	40 to 35
11	Above 40

The USDA Plant Hardiness Zone Map is useful for selecting plants from gardening catalogs, but it doesn't take into account important factors such as snow cover, precipitation and humidity, sunlight, seasonal winds, or *microclimates*. *(Courtesy of Agricultural Research Service, USDA)*

Department of Agriculture (USDA) Plant Hardiness Zone Map. The 1990 version of this map divides North America into twenty separate zones according to their average annual minimum temperatures. In an average winter, each zone is 5°F colder than its adjacent zone to the south. In Zone 3b, where I live, the coldest it usually gets in winter is -30°F to -35°F (-34°C to -37°C).

Mail-order garden catalogs often use the USDA zone map to tell their customers whether a particular plant can survive the winter in that customer's location. For example, the catalog from my fruit supplier tells me the Red Haven peach is hardy only to Zone 5. No sense trying to grow it in my much colder Zone 3. For such purposes, the USDA zone map is helpful, especially for gardeners on the eastern half of the continent.

But it does have its drawbacks. The USDA zone map considers only temperature. It ignores other factors that affect gardens: snow cover in winter, freeze-thaw cycles, precipitation and humidity, sunlight, and even seasonal winds. For many parts of North America, winter temperature lows are not the only significant aspect of climate that affects gardening.

Other zone maps try different approaches. Some base their zones on "ecoregions" that share similar native vegetation. Another, published by the American Horticultural Society, recognizes that summer heat can limit plant survival as much as winter cold.

To a large extent, however, all these plant hardiness zone maps concern *perennial* plants. They help gardeners understand which plants can survive summers *and* winters, year after year, in their garden location. This information will help the kitchen gardener grow certain herbs and fruits. But mostly, kitchen gardeners grow annual vegetables that aren't expected to survive winter. So, in that sense, you needn't care how cold it gets in January. By then, your crops have long since gone into the root cellar or the compost bin. Knowing what zone you're in isn't all that helpful.

Frost Dates

Instead, you need to know something else about where you garden, about your climate. You need to know, first of all, your *frost dates*. By this I mean the date of the last frost in spring and the date of the first frost in fall.

The date of the last spring frost tells you when it's usually safe to set out your tender plants, such as tomatoes. These are plants that would be damaged or even killed by frost. So it's important that you

and lilac leaves ...
Black flies very hungry.

May 4
Began hardening off onion plants.
Seeded more spinach & arugula.

May 10
Harvested first asparagus — delicious!

May 11
Planted out 585 onion plants.

May 17
Prepared 40' row for muskmelons —
row covers, wire hoops, black water jugs.
Began hardening off melons.

May 24
Seeded more greens in back bed.

May 26
Full moon + frost last night — everything
covered. Planted out melons under

Good gardeners are habitual record keepers. Over time, keeping track of first and last frosts and other dates will provide you with invaluable data.

not plant them unprotected in the garden until the danger of frost has passed.

The last spring frost is also a sort of benchmark for your garden planning. It helps you set your gardening schedule for the whole season. For example, if you grow your own tomato plants indoors, you'll use this date to decide when to start the seeds in early spring. You'll count back, say, four weeks from the date you expect the last spring frost. By timing the start of your seedlings in this way, you can be sure they'll be just the right size to go out into the garden as soon as the danger of frost has passed. But even if you buy plants at your local nursery or farmers' market, you'll still need to know when it's safe to set them in your garden.

So the date of the last spring frost is the first thing you must know about your climate. It's part of the answer to that question, Where am I?

Every gardener also needs to know what date to expect the first frost in fall. You must keep this date somewhere in the back of your mind. It's a sort of deadline—from this date on, you'll have to be prepared for frost. It helps you draw a boundary around your growing season just as a fence forms a boundary around your vegetable plot.

Of course, at best you only come up with the *usual* dates of the last spring frost and the first fall frosts. The actual dates will vary somewhat from year to year. I know that *usually* my garden isn't hit by frost after Memorial Day and then not again until early September. But as I've mentioned already, Jack Frost has visited my garden in every month of the year. So I have to stay alert. In the coming chapters, you'll learn to forecast and fend off frosts so you won't be caught off guard.

How do you learn the frost dates for your area? A lot of statistical information about weather and climate is available to us these days. The Internet can be a useful tool for finding this. Your local cooperative extension office can also help. (See Appendix 3 for more about these resources.)

Just be aware of the difference between *usual* frost dates and *average* frost dates. The average spring frost date means that half the time the last frost of spring strikes *before* that date and half the time the last frost strikes *after* that date. Such information isn't very useful unless you don't mind getting frosted half the time.

To get a handle on the usual frost dates for your locality, don't forget the best and most obvious resource: your gardening neighbors. The frost dates that your neighbors tell you over the back fence will likely be more helpful to you than those gotten over the World Wide Web. At least your neighbors' dates will be good starting points, and you can refine them as you gain experience in your own garden.

Good gardeners are always record keepers— whether those records are kept on paper or in the memory. So you'll want to note these frost dates somewhere each year. Before long, you'll know your gardening season the same way a football fan knows when the playing season begins and ends.

Frost-Free Days

The next important thing to know about your climate is its number of *frost-free days*. This is simply the number of days between your last spring frost and your first fall frost. It is the total number of days you can reasonably expect to have of frost-free gardening. Again, this will vary from year to year, and some years Jack Frost will pay you a surprise visit or two. But the number you come up with will give you a good clue about which vegetables will grow successfully in your garden. It will, in a sense, define your growing season (although later on we'll discuss ways to extend that season by artificially creating more frost-free days).

In my garden, I can usually count on no more than about 100 frost-free days. So if I'm considering growing a tender vegetable variety that takes (according to the seed catalog) 120 frost-free days to mature, I'd better think again. At the very least, I will need to employ some season-extending methods to help this vegetable along. That's why the total number of frost-free days is an important thing to understand about your garden climate.

With experience, you may find that the frost dates for your own garden are surprisingly different than those of some of your neighbors. A man who gardens only a quarter mile away from me regularly gets two or three more weeks of frost-free gardening than I do. That's because his garden is up on the sunny side of a wind-protected hill, while my garden is down in what we jokingly call "frost valley." On the USDA Plant Hardiness Zone Map, this man and I are in the

---

Microclimate:

The weather conditions of a specific small site as compared to the climate of the surrounding area. Factors affecting micro-climate:
- **elevation relative to surrounding area**
- **shelter from wind currents**
- **sun exposure**

---

same climate zone. But looked at more closely, we seem to be in substantially different climates.

The difference has to do with what gardeners call *microclimates*. The word refers to the particular weather conditions of a small site or habitat, such as a garden. The microclimate of my garden—in a low valley often buffeted by wind—is substantially different than the microclimate of this neighbor's garden, which is higher, sunnier, and more sheltered.

So getting acquainted with your *climate* must also mean getting acquainted with your *microclimate*. This is well worth the effort. You may learn, as I have, that you can't always trust the regional weather forecasts heard on the radio. What will be nothing more than a chilly September night elsewhere in my county often means frostbitten tomatoes in the microclimate of my garden.

I've also learned over the years about microclimates *within* my garden. I now know which corner of my garden gets the best wind protection and which beds get the most sunshine. I've noticed, too, that certain places are always the first to get hit by those light frosts that leave other areas of my garden untouched.

I began this chapter by saying that all gardening begins with a question: Where am I? I then suggested that to answer that question fully you must get acquainted with the climate where you garden. This is essential if you are to successfully garden with frost. You must know the frost dates for your garden and the number of frost-free days you can reasonably expect in a typical gardening season. You must also acquaint yourself with your microclimate—in your neighborhood and even within your garden boundaries.

Your gardening neighbors may be the best source of information about when to expect first and last frosts in your area.

Knowing where you are doesn't necessarily mean *accepting* all the limitations of your climate. You need to know the usual frost dates for your garden—but you don't have to be bound by them. After all, with a little forethought you can usually shepherd your garden safely through the light frosts of spring and fall. You'll learn how to do that soon.

But next we turn to what every cold-climate gardener needs to know about frost.

Chapter 2

Understanding Frost

Before we go any further, let's ask ourselves another question.

What is frost?

You've probably heard a confusing assortment of names for frost: hoarfrost, black frost, white frost, glazed frost, ground frost, air frost. Then there's freezing fog, rime ice, and frozen dew. Why all the names? Isn't frost, well, just *frost*? Isn't it that white stuff that you suddenly find covering your garden some fall morning, signaling the end of gardening?

Not exactly.

Let's imagine three different mornings in your garden. The first is the fall morning mentioned above. The night was chilly and now a feathery white blanket of tiny ice crystals covers the ground. Soon the plants you neglected to protect last evening will droop and blacken. No doubt about it, *that* was frost.

But let's imagine another morning. Again, the night was rather chilly, but now there's no white stuff on the ground. In fact, the ground is damp with dew. But later in the day you discover that all the blossoms on your beautiful young eggplants have fallen off. It hadn't *felt* cold enough for frost—so why this damage? Was *this* frost?

And now imagine a third cold morning. This one feels well below freezing. But in the garden there's no sign of that feathery white blanket. No "frost." Yet, when you stroll through the garden later, you're surprised to find blackened leaves on your tomato plants. Could *this* have been frost?

In all three examples, your garden was injured by cold. But only in one did you "see" that cold in the form of a cover of white ice crystals that we typically call frost.

Frost:
Frost is the sudden and untimely onset of temporary freezing temperatures that injure your garden plants during the gardening season.

Chill Injury:
Damage to a plant resulting from cold, but not freezing, temperature.

So what *is* frost?

First of all, we should understand that different gardeners use different definitions of frost. What one gardener—or one gardening book—means by frost may be quite different than what another gardener or book means by frost. So before going further, let me tell you *my* definition—what I mean by frost when I'm writing about it in this book.

Frost is the sudden and untimely onset of temporary freezing temperatures that injure your garden plants during the gardening season.

This will be our working definition of frost in this book. We'll discuss it in more detail in a moment. But first, let's talk about some cold-related problems in the garden that are *not* frost.

Chill Injury

Take the example of the eggplant dropping its blossoms. This typically happens with eggplant when the temperature drops into the low forties (Fahrenheit—or into high single digits Celsius). On the morning we imagined in your garden, the temperature had fallen into the low forties but not below freezing. So, by our working definition, your eggplant had not been injured by frost. Instead, it had suffered what we could call a "chill injury."

Cold temperatures affect many inhabitants of the kitchen garden. In fact, air temperatures that hover just *above* freezing for a prolonged time can kill most tender plants.

Air temperature plays an important role in plant growth. It influences nearly every physiological process, from nutrient absorption to flowering and fruiting. Every plant species (and every new variety) has its own *critical temperatures*. This means the *minimum* and *maximum* temperatures between which a plant continues growing and the *optimum* temperature it needs for greatest growth. Each plant also has *lethal* temperatures, both high and low, at which that plant dies.

All of these critical temperatures may vary somewhat depending on the plant's stage of development. For example, seed germination may require one temperature, but other temperatures may be needed for vegetative growth or for flowering. Optimum temperatures may also vary between day and night. Tomatoes, for example, typically set fruit best at night temperatures in the sixties (Fahrenheit—that's the high teens Celsius). In fact, if nighttime temperatures do not fall below 72°F (22°C), tomatoes may begin to drop their blossoms.

So, as you can see, all air temperatures affect plants. But in this book we're interested particularly in freezing temperatures. Later you'll learn how to predict frost and how to protect plants from frost. Many of those methods will also work well for predicting the onset of cold temperatures in general and for protecting your garden from chill injury. Nevertheless, by our working definition, a "chill" is not a frost.

Frost Means Freezing

To understand frost, let's go back to our definition: *Frost is the sudden and untimely onset of temporary freezing temperatures that injure your garden plants during the gardening season.*

Note that, when we talk about frost, we're talking about something that happens "during the gardening season." Obviously, I don't wake up in February, notice that the overnight temperature was -26°F (-32°C), and say, "Oh, we had a frost." The frost we're talking about is "untimely" and "temporary" and it happens during the gardening season.

That said, notice that the most important word in our definition is *freezing*. In this book, freezing is what makes frost, frost. Temperatures above freezing may be chilly—they may even harm your garden. But that damage won't have been caused by frost. That damage was caused by chill injury.

Frost means freezing. And what do we mean by *freezing*? For practical purposes, freezing means 32°F (0°C) or lower. That's because most of us think of 32°F (0°C) as the temperature at which water freezes. Scientists would rather have us say that 32°F (0°C) is the temperature at which ice melts. They like to point out that, under certain conditions, water can be cooled *below* 32°F (0°C) without freezing. This is called *supercooling*.

But in the kitchen garden we needn't worry about this detail. In fact, our definition of freezing can be quite imprecise, because we will want to take protective action whenever it seems the temperature is going to drop to anywhere near "freezing."

So let's think of 32°F (0°C) as the "frost damage line." At or below this temperature, your garden can expect frost and damage. As you will soon learn, it's immaterial whether or not that familiar white coating is visible on your garden the next morning.

By our definition, frost occurs—and does damage—whenever the temperature in your garden falls to 32°F (0°C) or below. Perhaps, then, I should have titled this book "A Gardener's Guide to *Freezing*." I could have reserved the word *frost* to mean only the feathery white coating of ice crystals that sometimes appears during freezing temperatures. But gardeners customarily talk about "frost" when they're discussing the damage done by freezing temperatures. So in deference to gardening tradition, I'll use *frost* to mean *freezing*.

Some gardeners refine the definition of frost a bit further. They call it a *light frost* when the temperature drops to between 32°F and 29°F (0°C and -2°C); a *moderate frost* when the temperature is between 28°F and 25°F (-2°C and -4°C); and a *severe frost* when the temperature falls below 25°F (-4°C). Generally, I'll simply use *frost* to mean any temperature of 32°F (0°C) or lower.

How Frost Hurts

How exactly does frost do its damage? How does frost hurt? Well, scientists aren't absolutely sure. As researchers Akira Sakai and Walter Larcher have written in their book *Frost Survival of Plants* (Springer-Verlag, 1987): "Of the manifold hypotheses and theories that have been propounded over the years [about how freezing kills plants], none has proved entirely satisfactory." Apparently, however, most fingers point at two culprits: dehydration and disturbance of the cell membranes.

Keep in mind that all of the following describes

Garden plants may be damaged by cold, even when there is no visible coating of frost on your plants in the morning.

what is thought to take place deep *within* the plant tissue, invisible to the naked eye. In general terms, freezing causes tiny ice crystals to form on the surface of cells. This is called *extra*cellular freezing. When this happens, water is drawn out of the cells through the cell membranes. If the temperature drops slowly and does not drop too low, and if the freeze does not last too long, then uninjured cells will reabsorb the

Freezing apparently causes tiny ice crystals to form on the surface of cells within the plant tissue. Water is drawn out through the cell membranes. This dehydration can injure the plant unless water is reabsorbed during thawing. If the temperature drop is rapid and extreme, however, the water within the cells may freeze and rupture the cell membranes. These cells cannot recover.

water when they warm back up. But if the water cannot be reabsorbed, the plant can be injured or killed by this loss of water. This is dehydration.

A harder freeze also causes *intra*cellular freezing. Here the water *within* the cells freezes and may even burst the cell membranes. These cells cannot recover.

As I said, we can't see any of this with the naked eye, but we know the result: blackened, lifeless leaves and mushy, spoiled fruits.

So that explains what probably happens inside a plant when its temperature drops to freezing. Now let's try to explain what brings frost to our gardens. What makes the temperature drop to freezing?

How Frost Happens

In simplified terms, the sun warms the earth and, whenever the sun disappears, the earth begins to cool. This is called *radiational cooling*. The earth, in fact, is always losing heat through radiation, day and night. During the day this heat loss is more than offset by heat gained through solar radiation. But at night, in the sun's absence, the earth loses more heat than it gains. It will be coldest about daybreak.

If the earth loses enough heat at night, the temperature at ground level will drop below freezing and your garden will have a *radiation frost*. That's the most common way frost happens. It accounts for the light and moderate frosts that our gardens can usually survive if we protect them adequately.

The other cause of frost is the arrival of a huge mass of freezing air from somewhere else. For example, sometimes weather conditions bring polar air pouring down onto your area from up north. Think of it as a tidal wave of freezing air that suddenly engulfs your whole region. This causes what's called an *advection frost*. Thank goodness, this happens less frequently, because it kills everything but the hardiest plants. Usually the killing frost that comes in the fall and signals the end of your garden is an advection frost.

You can understand these two types of frost with the following analogy. One winter night you wake up cold because you have kicked off the bed covers. Without that blanket, you've been rapidly losing

Radiation Frost: Frost caused by cooling of the earth (heat loss) resulting in freezing temperatures at ground level.

Advection Frost: Freezing due to the arrival of a huge mass of freezing air, such as an arctic air mass.

body heat, and now you're shivering. That's like a radiation frost. The next night you wake up cold again. This time you've still got the blanket over you, but you've left the bedroom window wide open, and now a frigid wind is howling in, making you shiver again. That's like an advection frost.

With both types of frost, the temperature drops below freezing and your garden is damaged.

Frost and Humidity

To understand frost fully, you need to understand some things about *humidity*. As I'm sure you know, humidity refers to water vapor in the air. Let's look at four keys to understanding humidity and frost.

First, more water vapor can exist in warm air than in cold air. This fact sometimes leads people to say that warm air can "hold" more moisture than cold air; but air isn't a sponge that sops up moisture. Air doesn't "hold" water vapor in this sense. Nor is the atmosphere a motel with a certain number of empty rooms to fill, after which the "no vacancy" sign lights up. Warm air doesn't have more "space" in it than cold air.

Why then can more water vapor exist in warm air? In part because water molecules, when warm, move more rapidly than water molecules that are cold. And as water molecules move more rapidly, many of them change from liquid to gas—they become water vapor. So, generally speaking, warm air has more of these fast-moving molecules of water vapor, and cold air has fewer. It's a matter of speed, not space.

Where does this water vapor come from? Often, when warm air hovers above a source of water, some of that water enters the air as vapor. We call this *evaporation*. It's what makes your garden dry out on a sunny afternoon. The water in your soil is evaporating into the warm air.

Second, if this warm air cools, it will eventually reach a point of saturation. The amount of water vapor in this air will then be the maximum possible at its temperature and pressure. This air will be saturated.

Third, if this saturated air cools even further, the water vapor in it will begin changing back to liquid. We call this process *condensation*. In the cooler temperature, some water molecules will slow down and change from vapor to liquid. The same process causes that film of moisture to form on your cold glass of iced tea on a muggy August afternoon. The warm August air contacts your cold drink, and some of the water vapor in that air changes to tiny liquid droplets on the surface of your glass.

Fourth, the temperature at which this occurs is called the dew point temperature of that air—or simply its dew point. If this air is at ground level when it cools to its dew point, the water vapor in it will condense

---

Understanding Humidity and Frost

1. **More water vapor can exist in warm air than in cold air.**

2. **As warm air cools, it will eventually reach a point of saturation, that is, its maximum capacity of water vapor at that temperature and air pressure.**

3. **As saturated air cools even further, the water in it will convert from vapor to liquid.**

4. **The temperature at which this conversion takes place is called the *dew point*.**

---

into a thin layer of liquid water droplets on your garden—dew. Hence, the name dew point. Using an instrument called a sling psychrometer, meteorologists can determine the dew point temperature of air—before the dew forms. They can predict the temperature at which dew will form.

Note that this dew on your garden did not fall from the sky. It did not appear because of *precipitation*, as is the case with rain or snow. It appeared because of *condensation*. It formed because warm, moist air encountered a colder surface—your garden. This surface cooled the adjoining air down to its dew point temperature. Thus cooled, the water molecules slowed down and changed from vapor to liquid. Dew formed.

But how is dew related to frost? And why does Jack Frost sometimes leave his telltale white calling

When ice forms on the surface of plants as separate crystals, it gives this frost a feathery white appearance.

card and sometimes not? To answer these questions, let's look again at the various names for frost mentioned earlier.

Understanding Dew and Frost

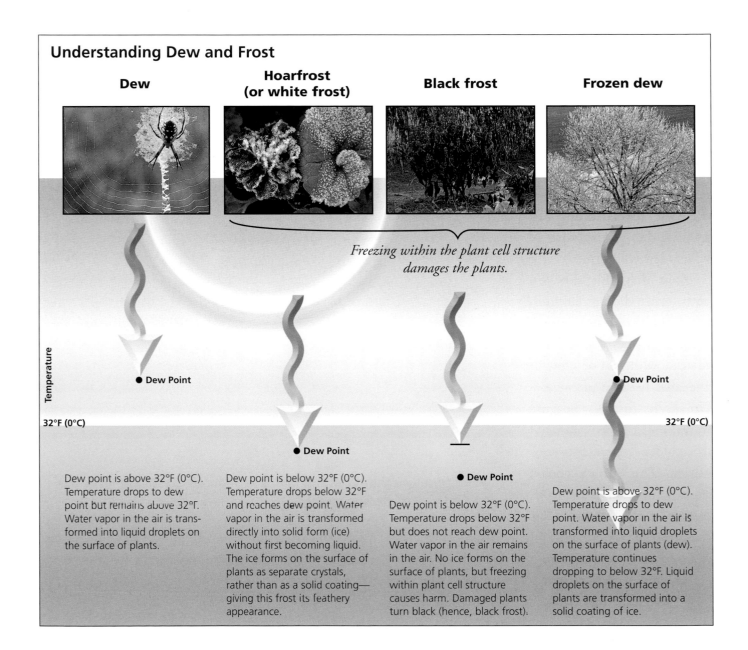

Dew

Hoarfrost (or white frost)

Black frost

Frozen dew

Freezing within the plant cell structure damages the plants.

Temperature

● Dew Point

● Dew Point

32°F (0°C)

● Dew Point

● Dew Point

● Dew Point

32°F (0°C)

Dew point is above 32°F (0°C). Temperature drops to dew point but remains above 32°F. Water vapor in the air is transformed into liquid droplets on the surface of plants.

Dew point is below 32°F (0°C). Temperature drops below 32°F and reaches dew point. Water vapor in the air is transformed directly into solid form (ice) without first becoming liquid. The ice forms on the surface of plants as separate crystals, rather than as a solid coating— giving this frost its feathery appearance.

Dew point is below 32°F (0°C). Temperature drops below 32°F but does not reach dew point. Water vapor in the air remains in the air. No ice forms on the surface of plants, but freezing within plant cell structure causes harm. Damaged plants turn black (hence, black frost).

Dew point is above 32°F (0°C). Temperature drops to dew point. Water vapor in the air is transformed into liquid droplets on the surface of plants (dew). Temperature continues dropping to below 32°F. Liquid droplets on the surface of plants are transformed into a solid coating of ice.

Frost Names

As the table on the opposite page shows, the names we give to frost will vary according to the circumstances. Remember that the dew point marks the temperature at which the air is saturated with water vapor, and it is the point at which condensation begins. This condensation will produce dew if the dew point temperature is above 32°F (0°C). But what if the dew point is below freezing?

If the dew point is below 32°F (0°C) and the temperature drops low enough to reach it, then the water vapor in the air transforms directly into a solid state (ice) without first becoming a liquid. No dew forms on the surface of the plants. Instead, ice forms there. This ice is actually composed of separate, tiny ice crystals—it's not a solid coating—and so it has a feathery white appearance. Most people call this *ground frost* or *hoarfrost* or *white frost*. It's what most of us think of when we hear the word *frost*. This is Jack Frost's white calling card.

Now let's look at another situation. Again the dew point is below 32°F (0°C), and again the tempera-

ture drops below freezing. But this time the temperature doesn't fall far enough to reach the dew point. The water vapor in the air remains in the air. Neither dew nor ice crystals form on the surface of the plants. If you looked out your window on a morning such as this, you might think there had been no frost—because there would be no visible "white frosting" on your garden. Nevertheless, because the temperature fell below 32°F (0°C), your tender plants experienced some freezing within their cell structures. The damaged plants will turn black. Hence, one name for this is *black frost*.

The final situation involves a progression. This time the dew point is above freezing. When the falling temperature reaches dew point, liquid droplets of dew form on the ground, but then the temperature continues falling—to below freezing. Now those liquid droplets on the surface of the plants freeze into a solid coating of ice—*frozen dew*. (Similarly, if fog freezes upon contact with a cold ground surface, it is called *frozen fog* or *air frost*. The resulting deposit of granular ice is called *rime ice*.)

Incidentally, *black frost* is not to be confused with *black ice*—a nasty traffic hazard caused by nearly invisible frozen or partially frozen dew or rain on the highway. And lest we feel too comfortable with these names, I should acknowledge that many regional differences exist. The British, for example, say frozen dew should be called hoarfrost. Any frost occurring with wind is, to them, a black frost, and the coating of ice that freezing rain leaves on trees and other upright surfaces they have named glazed frost . . . but never mind.

The thing to remember is that *freezing hurts plants* whether or not accompanied by some visible coating of ice—and whether or not we all agree on what to call it.

So dew point helps us understand why sometimes we see Jack Frost's calling card during a freeze and sometimes we don't. Later, dew point will help us gauge the possibility of a freeze, but for now just remember the important "frost damage line" of 32°F (0°C). By our working definition, anything at or below that temperature constitutes a frost.

Cold air runs downhill and pools in low areas and behind obstructions such as a wall or hedge.

How Frost Acts

They say that the first thing a plumber needs to learn is that water runs downhill (water, that is, along with anything else being carried in it!). Similarly, all gardeners need to learn that cold air runs downhill. In fact, it runs down the hill and over the rest of the landscape much the way a river of water does. Like

why the previous chapter empha-sized getting to know your location and its microclimates. A low spot on your property may collect cold air and become a "frost pocket"—not where you'd want to grow your garden. The foot of a hill is another likely spot for cold to settle. Understanding that cold air runs downhill will help you locate and lay out your garden in a way that avoids these cold air traps. The next chapter will go into more detail about planning a "frost-ready garden."

Humidity

To understand something else about how frost acts, let's return to our discussion of humidity. Remember that *humidity* refers to water vapor in the air.

water, cold air seeks the lowest ground. It collects as puddles of cold air in the low hollows, and it can get dammed up behind obstacles that block its downward path—just as water forms pools and gets backed up in reservoirs.

Where cold air goes, frost is sure to follow. That's

Why should a gardener care how much water vapor is in the air? Because the amount of water vapor in the air helps determine the rate at which the air temperature falls overnight. Generally speaking, the drier the air, the greater the drop in

temperature overnight (other things being equal). And the greater the drop in temperature, the greater the likelihood of an overnight frost.

Obviously, then, humidity is important to any gardener concerned about frost. So how can we best measure the humidity in the air?

Relative Humidity

Weather reports often mention *relative humidity*. This is a measure of how humid the air is at a certain temperature—compared to how humid it *could* be. It sounds simple, but this measurement can be deceiving.

Let's look at two separate parcels of air, one cool and the other warm. The temperature of one is 40°F (4°C), and the temperature of the other is 80°F (27°C). Let's say both parcels of air are as humid as they can possibly be at their own individual temperatures. That is, both have reached saturation, and both measure 100 percent relative humidity.

But are both equally humid? Do both have the same amount of water vapor in them?

Relative Humidity vs Dew Point

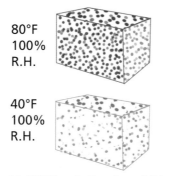

80°F
100%
R.H.

40°F
100%
R.H.

At 100% relative humidity, warm air (80°F) contains more water vapor than cooler air (40°F).

No, because, as we've learned, more water vapor can exist in warm air than in cool air. So in our example, the actual amount of water vapor would be greater in the warm (80°F) parcel of air than in the cool (40°F) parcel of air. The warm air would be significantly more humid than the cold air—even though our measurements would tell us that both parcels have a relative humidity of 100 percent.

Measuring relative humidity alone will give us a rather distorted picture of how much water vapor is in the air. What works better?

Dew Point

Dew point is a more helpful measurement of humidity, especially for gardeners. Unlike relative humidity, the dew point indicates how much water vapor is *actually* in the air. As I mentioned earlier, meteorologists determine the current dew point using a special instrument. These days weather reports often include the current dew point temperature.

Jack Frost's telltale white calling card.

Here's a simple rule of thumb for interpreting dew point:

A *low* dew point temperature indicates little actual water vapor in the air.

A *high* dew point temperature indicates an abundance of water vapor in the air.

To test this rule of thumb, let's return to our example of the two parcels of air—one cool and the other warm. Remember that we said both were as humid as they could possibly be at their own individual temperatures.

Remember, too, that the temperature at which a particular parcel of air becomes saturated is called its dew point temperature. Therefore, we know the dew point temperature of the cool parcel of air is 40°F (4°C) and the dew point temperature of the warm air is 80°F (27°C). We know that because both were as humid as they could be at these temperatures.

We have also already learned that the parcel of cool air has significantly less water vapor in it than the parcel of warm air. Do their dew point temperatures reflect this difference? Yes! The low dew point temperature (40°F) of the cool air tells us—correctly—that this air has little water vapor in it. And the high dew point temperature (80°F) of the warm air tells us—again, correctly—that this air has abundant water vapor in it.

So, you see, our rule of thumb works. It will work just as well in other situations. On another day, for example, that warm parcel of air might be much drier. It might have less than half as much water vapor in it. The temperature of the air could still be 80°F, but the dew point temperature would be much lower. And that low dew point would be our clue that this air is dry, not humid.

Low dew point temperature indicates dry air. High dew point temperature indicates humid air. In a later chapter, you'll learn how to use this information to predict whether or not your garden will get an overnight frost. But for our current discussion on how frost acts, let's try to see why humid air is less likely than dry air to bring frost.

Latent Heat

One reason why humid air is less likely to bring frost has to do with  the process of condensation. When water vapor in the air condenses into water droplets, a small amount of heat is released, which is called *latent heat*. This heat puts the brakes on the falling temperature. In fact, once significant condensation begins, the temperature normally will drop only a few more degrees.

Condensation begins; the latent heat slams on the brakes and slows the fall of the temperature. If this braking begins at a high temperature (as it would when the dew point is high), it has a good chance of stopping the temperature drop before it falls to 32°F (0°C). In addition, any fog created by the condensation will reflect back the heat radiating from the earth. The fog will act as an insulating blanket to inhibit heat loss from the earth.

But if the braking caused by latent heat begins at a lower temperature (as it would when the dew point is low), then the temperature will more likely skid all the way down past freezing. There goes your garden.

Here's a picture of a humid evening with a high dew point temperature. The air temperature begins to fall but very quickly reaches that high dew point. At this relatively high temperature, condensation takes place and, in the process, releases heat. This latent heat slows the drop in air temperature—probably enough to prevent frost.

Now here's a picture of a not-so-humid evening with a low dew point temperature. The air temperature begins to fall—and it continues to fall unimpeded

Fog acts as an insulating blanket that reflects back the heat radiating from the earth.

for a long ways until at last it reaches that low dew point temperature. Condensation finally takes place, releasing heat and slowing somewhat the drop in air temperature. But by now the air temperature is already quite low—and probably can't be slowed enough to prevent a frost.

So you can see that the *dew point temperature suggests the rate at which the air temperature will fall during the night*. Understanding this will be of great use to you later, when you learn more about predicting frost.

Lakes and Seasons

Here's another thing to keep in mind about water and the way frost acts. Large bodies of water, such as rivers and lakes, tend to change temperature more slowly than the surrounding land. In fact, water must absorb five times as much heat as dry land in order to increase its temperature the same amount, according to Jane Taylor in her book *Weather in the Garden* (Sagapress, 1996). Because of this, rivers and lakes exert a moderating influence on the local climate. They warm up slowly in spring, but they often remain warm long into fall. So, in the fall, they can share with a nearby garden their warmth and humidity, both of which can prevent frost. The moisture may even form a protective fog blanket over the shoreline areas.

Seasonal Differences

Finally, keep in mind that various seasonal differences will affect the way frost acts. Think about how the temperature of your soil changes with the seasons. In spring, your soil is still trying to shake off the deep cold of winter, but by fall, it has baked all summer in the hot sun. So your garden may be warmer on a fall night than on a spring night—because of the soil temperature. Autumn's advantage may be offset somewhat by the fact that fall soil often lacks the moisture content of spring soil—moisture that can raise the humidity of the microclimate of your garden. And humidity, as we have learned, can help inhibit frost. But, generally, fall soil will help protect your garden more than spring soil.

Day length can also play a role. Spring days are stretching longer as the weeks progress toward solstice, but fall days are getting shorter and shorter, with less warming sunshine. And fall nights are getting longer and longer—meaning more sunless hours during which the garden will cool.

Weather patterns in general will also differ between the seasons. The bottom line: A spring frost won't necessarily act the same as a fall frost.

Now that we understand something about frost—how it hurts plants, how it happens, and how frost acts—let's try using our knowledge to plan a garden that's ready to take on frost!

Chapter 3

Planning Your Frost-Ready Garden

The best time to begin preparing for frost is long before the first seed goes into the ground. In fact, you should think carefully about frost before you turn over that first spadeful of soil in your new garden. But even if that day has long past and your garden is well established, you may still be able to make some modifications to help transform it into a "frost-ready garden."

An important consideration for the frost-ready garden is siting. That means, where will you locate your garden? The key is to lay it out in such a way as to make the most of your microclimates. Here's when knowing "where you are" comes in handy. As you come to understand where you are, you'll understand more about frost in your garden.

53

Let's look at several important considerations in siting your garden.

Aspect

Aspect refers to the slope of your land and the direction of that slope. The best frost-ready garden has a gentle slope that faces south. This aspect gives the garden more direct sunlight during spring and fall, when frost can be a problem.

Keep in mind that the sun warms the soil faster and more deeply when its rays shine down perpendicular to the earth, instead of at an angle. That's because at an angle the rays must travel through more of the earth's atmosphere. By the time they strike the earth, some of their capacity to warm the soil has dissipated. The more deeply warmed the soil, the longer it will retain its heat on a cold night. That heat may be enough to save your garden from frost.

The sun works for the garden most effectively when it passes directly overhead, as it does in summer when it travels high across the sky. But in spring and fall, the sun travels lower across the sky, and its rays strike the garden at an angle. At this angle, the sunrays don't do as good a job warming the soil. Too bad, since that's when we need that warmth to help fend off frost.

This northern garden benefits from a south-facing slope. The superb aspect is further enhanced by terraces, so the soil warms quickly in the spring sunlight.

If you could just tilt your soil up a bit during those months, then the sunshine would strike your garden more directly, as it does in summer. Your garden soil would warm faster in spring and stay warm longer into fall. Increasing the slope of your garden would be like moving your garden south to a warmer climate.

You can do this on a small scale when you plant your seeds. Hoe soil into small "hills" for squash seed, and heap it into a long narrow ridgeline for a row of beans. The angled sides of this mounded earth will act as miniature solar collectors, warming the soil.

Unfortunately, you can't easily change the slope of your entire property. So instead look for a spot that already tilts toward the sun's path through the southern sky. This is the best aspect for a frost-ready garden.

Exposure

Next consider *exposure*, keeping in mind that there's "good" exposure (sunshine) and "bad" exposure (howling wind). A kitchen garden prefers full sunlight all day long. It also wants protection from being blown ragged and dried out by the prevailing winds. In an ideal site, you wouldn't have to cut down any trees or shrubs to ensure ample sunlight for your garden. Instead, just the right trees and shrubs would already be growing where they'd act as perfect windbreaks. They wouldn't be close enough to cast shadows or to steal soil nutrients and moisture from the garden.

But perhaps you don't have a perfect, ready-made site. In that case, windbreaks can often be grown (hedges), constructed (stone walls), or temporarily erected (snow fences). The best windbreak is short on the windward side and taller on the leeward side. In other words, the wind first hits something low, such as shrubs, and then hits something higher, such as trees. This slope deflects the wind up and over your garden. Such a windbreak can provide shelter for a distance of about seven times its height in very windy locations. The protection in less windy sites can even reach twelve times the height of the windbreak. Make your windbreak somewhat permeable rather than solid. A solid vertical wall can create fierce updrafts and

A stone wall may provide wind protection and also hold the heat of the day, releasing it slowly during the night.

swirling eddies that intensify the wind's damage.

Before you construct any windbreak, read ahead to the section on air drainage. You wouldn't want your windbreak to inadvertently trap cold air in your garden.

By the way, just because a south-facing slope is good, don't think that a hilltop is better. Yes, low spots collect cold, but high altitudes can be cold, too. In fact, temperature generally drops 3°F to 5°F with every 1,000-foot climb in altitude.

If you find yourself saddled with a less-than-ideal location—like all the rest of us—don't despair. Find some way to get at least six hours of full sun and plunge ahead.

Heat Reservoirs

Certain kinds of windbreaks can double as *heat reservoirs*, another important element of the frost-ready garden. Heat reservoirs absorb the sun's warming rays during the day and then slowly radiate heat at night. It's sort of like sleeping in a cold room with a cat curled at your feet. Your toes stay toasty warm all night.

A stone wall makes a good heat reservoir, as do stone out-croppings or big rocks. Buildings, especially dark-colored ones, have a similar effect. The ideal kitchen garden would have these heat reservoirs situated where they'd block arctic winds and absorb sunshine without shading the vegetables. Asphalt driveways reserve a lot of heat, too, although they don't block wind.

As we learned in the previous chapter, bodies of water can also be good heat reservoirs, especially in the fall. At that time of the year, they will stay warm even after the nighttime air temperature has dropped. They can share their warmth and humidity with your garden.

On a smaller scale, you can simulate this effect by setting out clear glass bottles filled with water dyed black. Use a few drops of food coloring or ink. Gallon wine jugs work well, especially those made of dark glass. Place the bottles strategically among your peppers and other heat-loving plants. Barrels of water also make good heat reservoirs, as well as providing a handy place to fill your watering can.

Site Considerations:
- **Aspect (gentle slope that tilts the garden to the sun)**
- **Exposure (sun= good; wind=bad)**
- **Heat reservoirs (structure that holds heat)**
- **Air drainage (escape route for cold air)**

Air Drainage

I mentioned howling wind and the harm it can do to plants, but air movement in itself isn't always bad. As we'll see later, moving air can often prevent frost on a nippy night. In fact, on such a night, a steady wind can be better than cold air that doesn't move at all, that gets trapped somewhere in your garden and can't move on. That's why the frost-ready garden needs *air drainage*.

Picture, again, a river flowing over your garden, headed toward lower ground. Ask yourself if the water will get dammed up anywhere within your garden—behind a stone wall, a hedge, or even behind a row of trees. If so, you have a problem with air drainage because the air, just like the imaginary river, will collect behind that "dam." In spring and fall when that air is especially cold, the result can be frost.

The solution is to "open the sluice way" of that dam. Create an opening in the wall or hedge so the cold air can drain away from your garden.

You can also create barriers that divert the flow of cold air before it reaches your garden. In effect, place a dam at the upper end of your garden so cold air can't enter. Construct it at an angle so the cold air keeps flowing but is shunted off to the side.

Just remember that *some* air movement is often helpful in a garden—not only to prevent frost but also to inhibit disease during a rainy, soggy summer.

Irrigation

The next consideration—*irrigation*—arises when the garden is *not* soggy. Plants that have their water needs met are a bit better prepared to withstand frost. Perhaps that's because frost, in part, harms plants by dehydrating them. Plants that are already thirsty are more susceptible to dehydration.

Of course, every garden needs a handy source of water—for helping seedlings in the spring and for enduring the occasional dry week. The frost-ready garden simply has an additional reason for keeping the vegetables watered properly.

Soil

Similarly, every garden needs good *soil*, but the frost-ready garden needs it even more. Gardeners speak of

tilth—the physical structure of the soil and its suitability for growing crops. A soil rich in organic matter has good tilth. It welcomes plant roots, it contains the nutrients plants need, and it holds water without being soggy—just the medium needed to keep plants properly watered in the frost-ready garden.

In addition, black loamy soil absorbs the sun's rays and warms more quickly than a light-colored sandy soil. Good gardeners constantly improve their soil anyway. The frost-conscious gardener gets double duty out of the improvements.

Beds

One further thing you may want to do with your soil: consider building *raised beds*. They won't, in themselves, prevent frost from hitting your garden, but in cold-climate areas, they're a good way to extend your already short season. In the spring, they warm faster and dry out earlier so you can begin planting sooner. They also give you an opportunity to use a *modular* system in your garden. That is, make the beds identical in size and shape so that a frost-protecting covering that fits one bed will fit them all. This will make life easier for you on those chilly nights when you're scrambling to get everything covered.

If your garden is sloped enough, consider building permanent *terraces*. Wooden or stone "risers" in a terraced garden will catch sunlight if facing south. That will provide extra warmth for low crops (such as spinach and lettuce) planted in front of the risers. You can also stretch clear plastic sheeting from riser to riser, thereby capturing even more warmth.

One gardener I know leaves a special place in her garden for what she calls a *manure trench*. In the spring, she digs a long trench the width and depth of her spade blade. She piles the soil from this trench in two long hills that run along both sides of the trench. Then she fills the trench with horse manure and plants her seedlings in the long narrow hills alongside the trench. All of this is enclosed using wire hoops and slitted row covers (transparent plastic sheeting with slits for ventilation). The manure provides heat as well as nourishment, and the row covers

Lettuce, leeks, Egyptian onions and garlic resume growing in the spring after dormant winter.

probably be one of the first things you can bring to your dinner table in the spring. So site that bed in a spot where it will thaw and warm up early.

In all of this, keep in mind that not many of us garden on "perfect" garden sites. To a certain extent, we all make do with what's available. The point is to come up with the best combination of aspect, heat reservoirs, air drainage, and so forth. Then start gardening. You'll soon learn other things you can do to help offset some of the disadvantages of your garden site. Here are some more suggestions for planning your frost-ready garden.

provide protection (to 22°F [-6°C], she claims) without overheating the plants. Using this method, she plants as soon as the snow melts. (If you take this approach, be sure to wash the resulting vegetables throughly as a precaution against any E. coli bacteria in the manure.)

While laying out your beds, think about where to locate any perennial crops you plan to have in your kitchen garden. Asparagus, for example, will

Seed Varieties

Choose your seed varieties carefully. No sense wasting time on something that can't possibly mature in the length of your season. Also note that the number of "days to maturity" cited in the seed catalogs may assume warm, sun-drenched days—not the nippy kind where you live. Plant growth and development are influenced by warmth, not just by the passage of time. So the "days to maturity" will

Peas are a good choice for early planting. They don't mind frost before they set flowers.

vary according to the accumulated mean temperatures of those days. Once again, the best idea is to consult with other gardeners near you. What varieties work best for them?

Speaking of varieties, you'll have a much wider selection to choose from if you start your own plants indoors rather than buying only what's available at the local garden center. Your windowsills may be sunny enough for this. If not, use lights. Don't assume that you need expensive "grow lights" and a fancy setup. At my house, I use ordinary shop lights with cool-white fluorescent bulbs set to a timer. They hang from a simple wood frame set up in the basement. The seedlings grow like mad. You could even set a shop light atop two low stacks of books and place your seedlings on the floor between the stacks. As the plants grow taller, add more books to the stacks.

Here's another advantage of growing your own seedlings. Since I never know for sure what kind of spring weather to expect, I sometimes start three "generations" of tender plants, particularly tomatoes. I time my main crop of tomato seedlings so they'll be ready to go into the garden on the usual, first, frost-free day. But I also start a few tomatoes a bit earlier—just in case we are blessed with an unusually warm spring. Then I can pop these into the ground early, without worrying that I'm risking my main crop. I may be rewarded with some extra-early tomatoes. I also start a few late seedlings to have as replacements in case an unforeseen frost kills some of my main crop.

With some vegetables, the variety you choose will depend on the "frost season"—spring or fall. Take peas, for example. Pea plants don't mind frost before they begin flowering. (Young plants can sometimes withstand temperatures as low as 17°F [-8°C].) But once they've flowered, even a light frost can prevent pods from setting. This works out fine in the spring, since the weather is usually settling down by the time the flowers appear. But in the fall, frosty weather is moving in just when the flowers and pods are forming. How can you protect a four-foot-high trellis of unruly pea plants?

Shepherd Ogden, founder of The Cook's Garden seed company in Vermont, solves this problem with a careful choice of pea variety. He grows Novella peas in his fall kitchen garden. This bush variety needs no trellis because the plants are low and self-supporting. Shepherd grows them in close, triple rows. Then whenever a fall frost threatens, he can easily throw a row cover over his pea plants to protect them.

Every spring I try to remember that frost is an inevitable part of gardening in a short-season area. As a friend of mine insists, "If you don't freeze something, you're not a good gardener!" Now that you have your frost-ready garden planned and planted, let's learn how we can predict when Jack Frost is going to pay you a visit.

Chapter 4

Forecasting Frost

Most of us gardeners rely on the forecasts of professional meteorologists for our frost warnings these days. After all, they have satellites, radar, and sophisticated instruments to help them make their predictions. So we listen to the weather reports on radio and television. In addition, a growing number of us keep track of weather conditions by means of the Internet. With whole television channels and websites devoted to the weather, we have a vast array of information available to us. (See Appendix 3 for a partial listing of sources.) All of this can be of great educational value to you as a gardener. And it can give you a reliable picture of what's happening in your regional *macro*climate.

By now you know that your garden has its own *micro*climate. You realize that the weather forecast for your *region* may not be a reliable prediction of what will happen in the *microclimate* of your garden. Though it may be comforting if the professional forecasters don't mention the word *frost* in their evening broadcast, you can't always depend on their predictions alone. It's not *their* tomatoes in your backyard.

Interpreting Regional Forecasts

I suggest that you keep an ear tuned to these regional forecasts—but keep your eyes on what is developing in your own local climate. Experience will teach you how to interpret the professional forecasts. For example, I've learned

that when the regional forecast on my radio calls for frost in the nearby Adirondack Mountains, I can expect it in my garden as well. Though I'm not up there in the cold mountains, my garden is in a cold "frost valley" that seems to be on the same "frost schedule" as the Adirondacks. So even when the forecast for my locality doesn't mention frost, I wait to hear what's in store for the mountains. I've learned to customize the regional forecast to better suit me.

You may discover similar parallels between your garden and other areas. Perhaps you'll find that frost in an area one or two hundred miles northwest of you tonight almost surely means frost in your garden tomorrow night.

Even if you can't find a parallel like that, you can probably make some simple observations to help you refine the regional forecast. For example, compare the current temperature on your outdoor thermometer with that given just now on the radio report. Or compare your overnight low with the low reported on the radio in the morning. The differences may give you clues about how to adjust the radio forecasts to fit your backyard. Perhaps you'll learn to expect your own temperatures to be 5° warmer, or colder, than what the radio predicts.

It will help if you know exactly where these forecasts are originating. Where is the weather station whose instruments are reporting the temperatures, wind directions, etc.? How far is it from you? Is it in

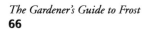

an urban area, but you live in the country? If so, the temperatures in the city will likely be warmer than yours. Maybe the station is at a higher elevation than you are. If so, its temperatures may be cooler. Or, if the weather station is downwind from you, the weather it predicts may well reach you earlier than forecast.

So evaluate these forecasts carefully. Their frost predictions may be right on the mark for you, or they may be unreliable. In any case, regional weather reports can at least alert you to the general weather conditions developing in your area. And with some practice, you can learn to spot the weather patterns that typically precede a frost.

Here is the way that climatologist Dr. James J. Rahn, author of *Making the Weather Work for You* (Garden Way, 1979), has described a typical weather pattern leading up to a frost. A low-pressure system, accompanied by mild weather, is followed by the arrival of a cold front. As this front passes over, the winds shift to come from the north or west. Showers may fall, but the first night stays mild as brisk winds and cloud cover prevent undue cooling. Then, over the next couple of days, the winds subside and the clouds depart. A high-pressure system is moving in behind the cold front. Now is the critical time for frost, during the second or third night after the cold

When the air is crisp and the horizon is sharply defined, be alert to the possibility of frost during the coming night.

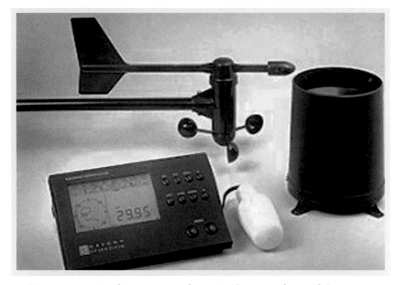

You can get a home weather station, such as this one from Oregon Scientific, but with careful observation and record keeping, you can learn to predict frost accurately without going to this much expense.

To help you make this call, you *could* invest in one of the computerized home weather stations now on the market. They are compact, apparently easy to use, and reportedly reliable. Wireless models are quick to install and some can take readings at remote locations—in your garden, for instance. Some are solar powered; some will alert you whenever temperatures fall below a level you determine. And most of them, as you might imagine, are quite expensive.

There is another way. Though the prospect of making your own forecast without computerized instruments may seem daunting, you can learn some simple guidelines that will help. Yes, forecasting the weather is an incredibly complicated science. I'm certainly grateful for the professionals who devote themselves to this difficult and often thankless enterprise. Those of us who garden would be foolish to ignore their predictions altogether.

I'm merely suggesting that you can increase your gardening fun if you do more than just tune in the television. You can teach yourself to tune in to the earth. You can learn a simple routine—a mental checklist to go through—that will help you make a surprisingly reliable forecast of frost.

You won't need fancy instruments. A minimum-

front has moved on. If you can make it past this, the "high" will move through your area and bring back warmer nights.

Making Your Own Forecast

Even after consulting the radio, the television, and the Internet, the moment will arrive when you must apply these forecasts to your own garden. Will your garden get frost tonight? Should you cover up?

maximum thermometer is fairly inexpensive and quite useful—but most any thermometer will do. A sling psychrometer costs a lot more, but you can use a homemade version that will suit your purposes just fine. You'll also need to keep a few records somewhere. Most gardeners already do that anyway.

I'll cover all of this in more detail later. For now, just realize that the most important thing needed for forecasting is not sold in any store. It also happens to be the most important thing needed in gardening. *You must learn to watch. You must learn to notice things.* It sounds simple, but these days it's a dying art.

Now let's get to that mental checklist for predicting frost.

Frost Dates and Season

Stay aware of your gardening calendar. Note how close you are to your garden's frost dates. If you've done your homework and gotten acquainted with your climate, you already have a general idea of when to expect frost in both the spring and fall.

Of course, frost can arrive at unexpected times.

One year I had an unusually early fall frost in August and an unusually late spring frost the following July—frost in every one of twelve consecutive months. Nevertheless, I know that in most years my "frost alert" times are June and September. That's when I must be alert for the warning signs of frost. Be aware of your "frost alert" times.

Keep in mind that spring and fall are quite different seasons in the garden. These differences relate to frost in some significant ways. Remember that nights are longer in the fall then in the spring—perhaps by as much as two hours. Those long fall nights will be more prone to cold and frost. And your soil is different, too. Usually, spring soil is cold but moist; fall soil is warm but often dry. Your soil's temperature and its moisture content will affect the microclimate of your garden. Warm, moist soil can help fend off frost.

Finally, remember that the plants in your garden will also be different in spring and fall because they'll be in different stages of their life cycle. In spring, many plants are in the most sensitive period of growth. They are sprouting or flowering or just starting to grow. Many young seedlings, still getting used to life out of doors, are especially sensitive to spring cold. Tomatoes, peppers, and eggplants come to mind. Lettuce, in contrast, doesn't mind a nip in the air when it's in its youth, but (like many of us) it requires a bit more coziness as it gets older. In other words, usually lettuce seedlings can take a frost; lettuce heads cannot. Similarly, young pea plants don't mind frost until they begin flowering. Springtime suits their schedule just fine, but in fall, peas will need protection on frosty nights.

Phase of the Moon

Now that you've taken into account the season, narrow the time frame a bit further. That is, for the next item on your mental checklist, notice what time of the month it is; specifically, be aware of the moon's phases.

For some reason, frost is more likely in the week before a full moon. Some gardeners report the same likelihood of frost under a new moon. Many meteorologists scoff at this bit of country wisdom, but Calvin Simonds, in his book *The Weather-Wise Gardener* (Rodale Press, 1983), offers the following explanation:

> *The moon makes tides in the atmosphere, just as it makes tides in the ocean. Presumably, the moon makes the highest tides in the atmosphere at the new and the full moon. Frosts occur under high-pressure areas. A high-pressure area is sort of a tidal bulge in the atmosphere. Doesn't it seem reasonable that if the moon tide effect is added to the effects of a high-pressure area, that frost may be made more likely?*

I'm no scientist, and I don't know who is right, but, personally, I wait to set out my pepper plants until *after* the full moon in June. And I've often been glad I've waited.

Cloud Cover

Cloud cover can also tell you something about the likelihood of frost. Remember that a low mass of thick clouds stretching from horizon to horizon will lay over your garden as snuggly as the down comforter you pull up to your chin on a winter's night. The clouds will reflect back the heat radiating from the earth. Frost is unlikely under such a blanket, but even high clouds offer some protection.

Just remember that the sky may clear overnight. If that happens, your garden will feel the way you do when you accidentally kick off your down comforter—cold! So, as evening falls, watch carefully for any signs that the clouds are beginning to thin, break up, or move away. This is one time you'd rather not see a patch of blue in a gray sky!

Wind

Although we want the clouds to stay put, we want the air to move. When the air is still, it tends to form layers, with the coldest layer down at garden level. A wind, even a breeze, will agitate these layers and mix the warm air aloft with the cool air below.

Unfortunately, even a stiff breeze at sunset is no guarantee that the wind will keep blowing all night. It's a bitter irony that the same gale that blows the

Frost Profile:
By recording the temperature at a set time every evening, over time you will see a pattern emerge that can help you assess the likelihood of frost.

frost-protection covers off your plants in evening may desert you just when you need it most in the chilly morning hours. In this instance, the radio forecast may tell you whether to expect wind or calm overnight.

Temperature

While checking the regional weather forecast, you no doubt heard a temperature prediction. This is when you can convert that temperature to the one you've found more likely in your garden. But with your own thermometer, particularly with a minimum-maximum thermometer, you can do better than that. A minimum-maximum thermometer records the highest and lowest temperatures and preserves this information until you reset it.

With either kind of thermometer, you can develop a *frost profile* for your garden. Simply put, a frost profile gives you a picture of when frost happens in your garden. Usually this picture is in the form of a graph. By making simple recordings, you will over time develop a way of gauging the likelihood of frost as this relates to temperature.

In the easiest method, you simply record the

temperature at a set time each evening. Then the next morning note whether your garden got frosted that night. Choose an evening time that correlates with sunset—for example, a half-hour or fifteen minutes after sunset. This way all your observations will begin at the same point, when the earth starts to cool. Also be careful to adjust your observation time when you change your clocks between standard and daylight savings times. Keep your observations at the same "sun time."

After collecting such data for a while, you'll be able to chart which evening temperatures are most often associated with frost. You can even assign percentages of frost likelihood. Suppose frost occurred eight out of ten times when you observed 39°F (4°C) at sunset. The next time it's 39°F at sunset, you can say the likelihood of frost that night is 80 percent.

In his Pennsylvania garden, climatologist Dr. James J. Rahn uses this method. He has found that evening temperatures cooler than the low forties usually mean frost. But temperatures above the upper forties mean no frost. Canadian gardener Jennifer Bennett, author of *The New Northern Gardener* (Firefly Books, 1996), has found that in her garden, late afternoon temperatures below 36°F (2°C) usually mean frost, while those above 41°F (5°C) probably mean no frost.

When considering temperatures, be aware that the thermometer outside your window may read several degrees warmer than the temperature at ground level in your garden. The warmth and shelter of your house account for some of the difference. So does the thermometer's distance above the ground. Since the air often forms layers of varying temperatures, a distance of several feet can mean a significant difference in temperature.

Keep that in mind as you look at your own thermometer—and as you consider reports from a professional weather station. The thermometers at these official weather stations are mounted at a standardized height—exactly five feet (1.52 meters) above the ground. That's a lot higher than your garden.

Of course, temperature alone is a rather crude forecasting tool. You can improve on it somewhat by using a method suggested by Dr. Rahn. In *Making the Weather Work for You*, he describes how to predict frost by observing temperature *drop*.

He suggests recording two evening temperatures, one near sunset and the other several hours later. You might choose sunset and three hours later, for example. In this method, you will use the beginning temperature and the difference in the two temperatures. So if the temperature at sunset is 50°F and the temperature three hours later is 38°F, you will be working with 50°F and a 12° difference. (You can make the same calculations using Celsius.)

Now design a graph with the possible sunset temperatures along the horizontal axis and the possible differences in the two temperatures along the vertical axis (see the table above). Each night put a dot at the point where these two temperatures intersect. The next morning, record whether or not you had frost by writing

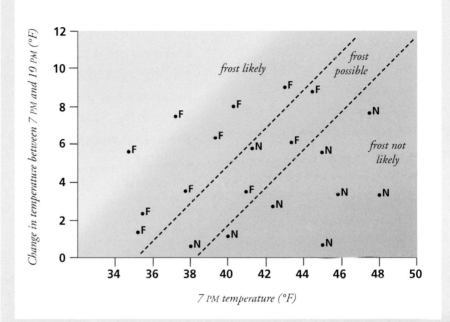

Forecasting Frost by Temperature Drop

frost likely

frost possible

frost not likely

Change in temperature between 7 PM and 10 PM (°F)

7 PM temperature (°F)

Graph the temperature at sunset with the amount of change three hours later, then note whether there was a frost that night (F or N). You will soon have a useful frost profile for your garden.

Source: James J. Rahn, *Making the Weather Work for You* (Charlotte, VT: Garden Way Publishing, 1979). Reprinted by permission of Storey Books, North Adams, MA.

either an *F* (frost) or an *N* (no frost) next to last night's dot.

As the dots take their places on the graph day after day, year after year, a pattern will emerge. Eventually, you'll be able to draw two lines (as shown), dividing the graph into three zones. The *frost-not-likely zone* will encompass the highest sunset temperatures and the least drops in temperature. The *frost-likely zone* will include the lowest sunset temperatures and the greatest plunges in temperature. In between will be the *frost-possible zone*—where sometimes it frosts and sometimes it doesn't.

Once you have determined these zones, you'll be able to begin forecasting frost. Simply note your two evening temperatures and plot a dot on your graph. Which zone does it fall into? Your main problem will be deciding what to do on evenings when the dot falls into that middle uncertain zone. To cover or not to cover?

If graphs aren't to your liking, try this formula suggested by a former British naval forecaster, David Bowen, in his book *Weather Lore for Gardeners* (Thorsons Publishers, 1978). Note the afternoon temperature at 3:30 p.m. and the evening temperature at 10:15 p.m. Calculate the difference between these two temperatures and multiply this number by

> **Bliss Formula:**
> At 1/2 hour after sunset, note air temperature (a) and dew point temperature (b). Add these temperatures and multiply the sum by .31 to get the lowest temperature likely (c).
>
> $$(a + b) \times .31 = c$$

two. Subtract that figure from the 3:30 p.m. temperature. The result, he says, is the likely temperature at about 5:00 the next morning.

All three of the above methods rely on temperature or temperature change to predict frost, but humidity provides another, more helpful, clue.

Dew Point

We learned in Chapter 2 that humidity tends to discourage frost by slowing the fall of air temperature. We also learned that the dew point temperature is the gardener's most useful tool for measuring humidity. The higher the dew point temperature, the more humid the air—and the less likely that the air temperature will plunge quickly to freezing. The lower the dew point temperature, the drier the air—and the more likely a precipitous drop in temperature that could mean freezing.

Sometimes dew point can help us predict a frost that we might not see coming by watching air temperature alone. Let's imagine two evenings. One is a warm 53°F (12°C), and the other is a cooler 42°F (6°C). Which night is more likely to have frost?

Before answering, let's imagine that the warm evening is dry, with a low dew point of 34°F (1°C). In contrast, the cooler evening has a higher dew point temperature of 40°F (4°C). That means the cooler evening is more humid. So, oddly enough, frost is more likely on the warmer evening—because of its lower humidity. We wouldn't know that from the air temperatures alone, but the dew point temperatures tell us the real frost story.

Dr. Rahn offers a rule of thumb for using dew point to predict frost. He suggests that a dew point temperature of 36°F (2°C) or lower at 9:00 p.m. means frost is likely. A dew point above 36°F at that time means frost is less likely.

Dr. Rahn also mentions another technique you might want to try. The Bliss Formula is used to predict overnight temperatures in the New Jersey cranberry bogs. Here's how it works. At a half hour after sunset, note the air temperature and the dew point temperature (in Fahrenheit degrees). Add these two temperatures together and multiply the sum by 0.31 to get the lowest temperature likely that night.

The data you collect about dew point and frost can be transferred to graphs, similar to those described above for tracking temperatures. The longer you collect data, the more useful this information will become.

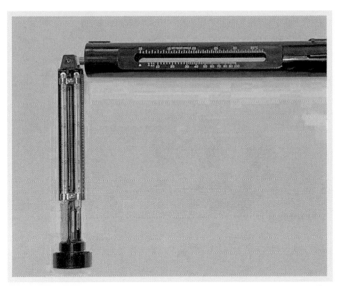

The sling psychrometer is a hand-held device used to measure humidity.

To accurately determine the dew point for your location, you need a hygrometer or a psychrometer, two instruments that measure humidity. The sling psychrometer is a hand-held devise consisting of two glass thermometers. The bulb of one is encased in a cotton wick soaked with water. The psychrometer is whirled around in the air. If the air is dry, the water evaporates around this "wet bulb thermometer," and its temperature drops. The difference in temperature between the wet bulb and the dry bulb thermometers depends on the humidity. That difference, called

Determining Dew Point Temperatures, °C

Dry Bulb (Air) Temperature, °C	Wet Bulb Depression, °C																					
	1	2	3	4	5	6	7	8	9	10	11	12	13	14	15	16	17	18	19	20	21	22
-20	-33																					
-18	-28																					
-16	-24																					
-14	-21	-36																				
-12	-18	-28																				
-10	-14	-22																				
-8	-12	-18	-29																			
-6	-10	-14	-22																			
-4	-7	-12	-17	-29																		
-2	-5	-8	-13	-20																		
0	-3	-6	-9	-15	-24																	
2	-1	-3	-6	-11	-17																	
4	1	-1	-4	-7	-11	-19																
6	4	1	-1	-4	-7	-13	-21															
8	6	3	1	-2	-5	-9	-14															
10	8	6	4	1	-2	-5	-9	-14	-28													
12	10	8	6	4	1	-2	-5	-9	-16													
14	12	11	9	6	4	1	-2	-5	-10	-17												
16	14	13	11	9	7	4	1	-1	-6	-10	-17											
18	16	15	13	11	9	7	4	2	-2	-5	-10	-19										
20	19	17	15	14	12	10	7	4	2	-2	-5	-10	-19									
22	21	19	17	16	14	12	10	8	5	3	-1	-5	-10	-19								
24	23	21	20	18	16	14	12	10	8	6	2	-1	-5	-10	-18							
26	25	23	22	20	18	17	15	13	11	9	6	3	0	-4	-9	-18						
28	27	25	24	22	21	19	17	16	14	11	9	7	4	1	-3	-9	-16					
30	29	27	26	24	23	21	19	18	16	14	12	10	8	5	1	-2	-8	-15				
32	31	29	28	27	25	24	22	21	19	17	15	13	11	8	5	2	-2	-7	-14			
34	33	31	30	29	27	26	24	23	21	20	18	16	14	12	9	6	3	-1	-5	-12	-29	
36	35	33	32	31	29	28	27	25	24	22	20	19	17	15	13	10	7	4	0	-4	-10	
38	37	35	34	33	32	30	29	28	26	25	23	21	19	17	15	13	11	8	5	1	-3	-9
40	39	37	36	35	34	32	31	30	28	27	25	24	22	20	18	16	14	12	9	6	2	-2

Dew point temperatures

Source (both pages): Edward Aguado and James E. Burt, *Understanding Weather and Climate* (Upper Saddle River, NJ: Prentice-Hall, 1999). © Reprinted by permission of Pearson Education, Inc., Upper Saddle River, NJ.

Determining Dew Point Temperatures, °F

Dry Bulb (Air) Temperature, °F	Wet Bulb Depression, °F																								
	1	2	3	4	5	6	7	8	9	10	11	12	13	14	15	16	17	18	19	20	21	22	23	24	25
0	-7	-20																							
5	-1	-9	-24																						
10	5	-2	-10	-27																					
15	11	6	0	-9	-26																				
20	16	12	8	2	-7	-21																			
25	22	19	15	10	5	-3	-15	-51																	
30	27	25	21	18	14	8	2	-7	-25																
35	33	30	28	25	21	17	13	7	0	-11	-41														
40	38	35	33	30	28	25	21	18	13	7	-1	-14													
45	43	41	38	36	34	31	28	25	22	18	13	7	-1	-14											
50	48	46	44	42	40	37	34	32	29	26	22	18	13	8	0	-13									
55	53	51	50	48	45	43	41	38	36	33	30	27	24	20	15	9	1	-12	-59						
60	58	57	55	53	51	49	47	45	43	40	38	35	32	29	25	21	17	11	4	-8	-36				
65	63	62	60	59	57	55	53	51	49	47	45	42	40	37	34	31	27	24	19	14	7	-3	-22		
70	69	67	65	64	62	61	59	57	55	53	51	49	47	44	42	39	36	33	30	26	22	17	11	2	-11
75	74	72	71	69	68	66	64	63	61	59	57	55	54	51	49	47	44	42	39	36	32	29	25	21	15
80	79	77	76	74	73	72	70	68	67	65	63	62	60	58	56	54	52	50	47	44	42	39	36	32	28
85	84	82	81	80	78	77	75	74	72	71	69	68	66	64	62	61	59	57	54	52	50	48	45	42	39
90	89	87	86	85	83	82	81	79	78	76	75	73	72	70	69	67	65	63	61	59	57	55	53	51	48
95	94	93	91	90	89	87	86	85	83	82	80	79	78	76	74	73	71	70	68	66	64	62	60	58	56
100	99	98	96	95	94	93	91	90	89	87	86	85	83	82	80	79	77	76	74	72	71	69	67	65	63
105	104	103	101	100	99	98	96	95	94	93	91	90	89	87	86	84	83	82	80	78	77	75	74	72	70

Dew point temperatures

The lower the dew point, the drier the air and the greater the likelihood of frost.

Before you proceed, consider this important word of caution about mercury thermometers, the typical glass thermometers sold in most stores. These thermometers contain liquid elemental mercury, a silvery white substance. Both the U.S. Environmental Protection Agency and Environment Canada have raised concerns about the toxicity of this mercury. If the thermometers break and the spilled mercury is not properly cleaned up, it can evaporate and harm both humans and wildlife. For this reason, at least one retail chain has withdrawn mercury thermometers from its store shelves, and some cities (including Duluth and San Francisco) have actually banned their sale. Alcohol thermometers (which contain a red or blue liquid) or galinstan thermometers (marked "mercury-free") are safer alternatives, though less easy to find.

the *wet bulb depression*, can be tracked on the tables on the preceeding pages to calculate the dew point temperature.

You can purchase a sling psychrometer or a computerized home weather station that will tell you the dew point (see Appendix 3), or you can easily make yourself a simple device that will help you determine the dew point. You will need an empty milk carton, a cotton shoelace (wide, as for an athletic shoe), some clear plastic tape, and two thermometers.

To make your device to determine dew point, cut off the top of the milk carton. Attach the two thermometers to two sides of the outside of the carton using the clear plastic tape so that you can still read their temperatures. Place them high enough so that you can cut a small hole beneath one of the thermometers, about an inch or two from the bottom of the carton. Carefully wrap one end of the shoelace around the bulb of this thermometer and thread the other end through the hole into the carton. Now pour water into the milk carton—high enough to soak the end of the shoelace but not high enough to drain out the hole you've cut in the side. The shoelace will wick up water from the carton and keep the bulb of its thermometer wet.

As the water evaporates from the shoelace wrapped around the wet bulb, this thermometer will register a temperature different from the other, dry bulb thermometer. You can track this difference on the table on pages 76–77 to calculate the dew point, much as you would with a sling psychrometer.

If you can't determine the dew point for yourself, check a professional weather report for your area. Calvin Simonds, in his handy

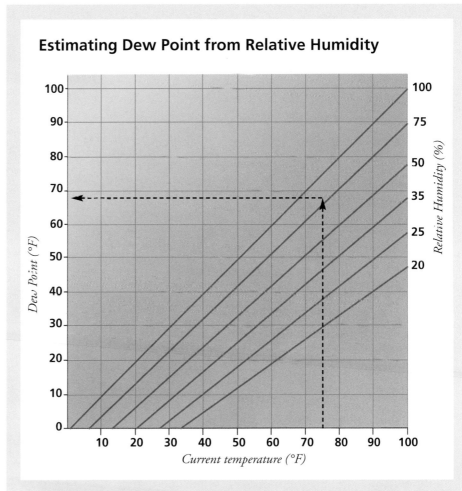

Estimating Dew Point from Relative Humidity

First, find your current temperature on the bottom scale. Then, move directly up until you hit the relative humidity line closest to your current relative humidity. Finally, go directly to the left-hand scale and read off your dew point. For example, if your temperature is 75° and the relative humidity is 80%, then the dew point is 68°.

guidebook *The Weather-Wise Gardener* (Rodale Press, 1983), says he doesn't worry much about frost if the dew point is above 45°F (7°C) on the six o'clock weather report.

Be aware that, as with air temperature, the dew point temperature for your garden may differ somewhat from this report because you're in a different microclimate. And, although dew point temperatures are more stable than air temperatures, they nevertheless can change between news time and nighttime.

If the weather report doesn't mention dew point, it may at least give the relative humidity. Take note of this and of your current air temperature. Then use the table on the preceding page (Estimating Dew Point from Relative Humidity) to estimate the dew point.

As an alternative, Dr. Rahn suggests that you simply note the air temperature when dew first begins to form on your lawn or garden in the evening. The lower this temperature, the greater the risk of frost. "If that temperature is above 40°F," says Dr. Rahn, "the danger of frost is slight." If it's below 40°F (4°C), prepare for frost. Of course, if the air happens to be quite dry, dew may not form before the temperature plunges below freezing. So if dew hasn't formed by the time the temperature has fallen to 40°F (4°C), expect frost.

Calvin Simonds notes another way to guess the dew point through observation:

If the air is murky and the horizon ill defined, if distant hills march away into a veil of haze, stars are indistinct and few in number, then you know the dew point is high. But if the atmosphere is lucid and distant hills are the same color as near ones, if you can see every detail of distant structures, if the sky is purply-blue at the zenith, if the sun sets to the horizon without changing color and the moon comes up the color of platinum and the stars come out in thousands, then you know the dew point is low. On such a night the wise tomato cringes.

Whatever method you use, the night will come when your best guess tells you to expect frost. What to do next is the subject of Chapter 5.

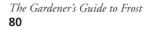

Fending Off Frost

Each year, as you prepare your garden, you know that sooner or later—in the spring or in the fall or in both—Jack Frost will pay you a visit. Knowing that, what can you do at the start of the gardening season to prepare for those frosty nights?

Preparing for Frosty Nights

You can do several things. First, remember this principle for all aspects of gardening: Healthy plants are the ones best equipped to take on trouble. That's true whether the trouble is disease, pests, or frost. Plants already under stress are the least ready to survive these problems.

In your garden, this means sturdy, healthy plants have a better chance of surviving frost

Timetable for Hardening Off Seedlings

	First Day	Second Day	Third Day	Fourth Day	Fifth Day	Sixth Day
In full sunlight						
Spindly plants	½ hour	¾ hour	1 hour	1½ hours	2¼ hours	3½ hours
Sturdy plants	1½ hours	2½ hours	3½ hours	5 hours	6 hours	7 hours
In light shade*						
Spindly plants	1 hour	1½ hour	2¼ hours	3½ hours	5 hours	3 hours in sun
Sturdy plants	2½ hours	3½ hours	5 hours	6 hours	7 hours	7 hours in sun

* Receiving reflected or indirect sunlight only for the first five days.

Source: Dorothy Hinshaw Patent and Diane E. Bilderback, *The Harrowsmith Country Life Book of Garden Secrets* (Charlotte, VT: Camden House Publishing, 1991). Reprinted by permission of the authors.

than the plants that are already struggling. In the spring, you can give them a good start by properly hardening off your seedlings before setting them out in the soil.

Hardening off is the process of helping your seedlings adapt to the change in light and temperature from the indoor environment where you started them to the outdoors where they will mature. You harden off seedlings by gradually exposing them to outdoor conditions. Each seedling must go through

a rather complex internal transformation as it adapts to the increased light and cooler temperatures. Be patient and allow enough time for this to happen (see table above).

A second way to give your plants a healthy resistance to frost is to keep them properly watered. As you will recall, one way frost hurts plants is through dehydration. Obviously, a plant that is already thirsty for water will be less prepared to survive further dehydration. In general, your kitchen garden needs an inch of water each week. If rain doesn't supply that much, you must make up the difference.

Finally, pay attention to your plants' nutrient requirements, particularly in the spring when growth is most rapid. Over-fertilizing, however, will be too much of a good thing, especially later in the summer. Nitrogen in particular promotes new, tender growth—which is more vulnerable to frost. So, as the seasons progress, be especially careful not to overfertilize perennials, which will need to go into winter dormancy. Some northern gardeners, in fact, stop fertilizing their perennials by July 1st to make sure the plants aren't prodded into harmful late season growth.

As soon as you set out your spring plants, have frost-protection covers handy.

As you set out your spring plants, consider the fact that all plants give off minute amounts of heat. Close planting can help retain this heat and may be beneficial to some crops. Peppers come to mind. They seem to thrive and become more productive when slightly crowded. Perhaps crowding helps warm these cold-sensitive plants.

As soon as I have plants in the ground, I make sure I also have my frost-protection covers ready. We'll discuss them in just a moment, but for now,

note that you'll want them handy, not hidden away somewhere in the back of the garage. Take a quick inventory of what you have and gather more if need be. If you laid out your garden with covering in mind (Chapter 3), your job of finding covers now will be easier. Remember that what works as a cover for small spring plants may not be large enough to adequately cover the sprawling, climbing plants of late summer.

What needs frost protection? The chart in

Unprotected, cold-intolerant flowers and vegetables are killed by the first hard frost. But with protection, many cold-hardy greens will survive well into winter.

Appendix 1 shows the frost tolerance of the various vegetables in a typical kitchen garden. It is designed to give you an easy way to see what's most vulnerable, what needs protection from the weather you're expecting. For easy reference, tack a photocopy of the chart to your garden shed door. If you can't find something on the chart, my suggestion is to cover it in any iffy situations. When in doubt, cover.

Lastly, if you have a big garden, as I do, you may want to jot down a list of what's currently in the garden that needs protection. I often find myself scrambling to cover the garden after dark, flashlight in hand. Occasionally, the next morning reveals some poor plant that got overlooked in the commotion. A list could save me from that mistake. I might even remember to make one next year.

Fending Off Frost

At last the gardening season has begun. Your seedlings have been properly hardened off and are now sturdy young plants. The germinating seeds are filling up their rows.

Meanwhile you're doing your weather

homework. Each day you consult the weather reports and go through your mental checklist for predicting frost. Now, this evening, you're certain: Jack Frost is on the way. Tonight's the night!

What do you do next? How do you protect your plants from frost?

Keep in mind a few of the principles we learned in Chapter 2 about how frost acts. First, remember that frost doesn't fall from the sky. We do not cover our plants to shield them from something that's going to rain down on them. Instead, we're trying to keep something *in*—heat. We want to *insulate* so as to *retain the heat* that is radiating from the earth.

Second, remember that, generally speaking, humidity inhibits frost. We want to enclose our plants in humid air. That humidity can put the brakes on dropping temperatures.

Of course, we all know that with a killing frost brought on by the influx of polar air—when temperatures plummet to well below freezing—you can't do much. Only the hardiest plants will greet you the next morning, but let's not get ahead of ourselves. We're talking now about those annoying light frosts that sneak up on us with just enough cold to damage

Half circles of wire fencing arched over rows to protect crops from deer also support bedsheets, synthetic row covers, or bubble wrap to keep frost off vulnerable and tender plants.

a good garden. With the right protection, your garden can survive those visits.

What Works

In the garden, the right protection means anything that will hold an insulating layer of warm air around your plants. Basically, the same sort of material that keeps *you* warm in cold weather will keep your garden warm. This includes anything from the traditional (blankets, tarps, sheets) to the newfangled (spun-bonded polypropylene row covers, thermal quilts).

All of these will work better if not laid directly on top of your plants. That's because these insulators are likely to get cold themselves, and plants in contact with them may be damaged. So try to create some space between plant and insulator. If possible, hold the covers aloft with wire hoops or other contraptions.

Plastic, being thin, makes for poor insulation. It also readily conducts the cold to whatever it contacts, so plants that touch it on a frosty night will likely be hurt. Plastic does do a good job, however, of holding in moisture. And clear plastic, if used in a tunnel, allows the sun's rays to warm the soil during the day.

Sometimes clear plastic is combined with water, as in "Wall o' Water" enclosures. These look like miniature teepees constructed of vertical, water-filled tubes. The water is warmed by the sun and helps protect young tomatoes or peppers.

A similar device is the cloche, invented by French market gardeners many years ago. *Cloche* is a French word for "bell." Some early cloches looked like glass bells set over plants. Other cloches, made of glass panes on wire frames, looked like miniature greenhouses. Called Chase cloches, they could be con-

Sunshine warms the water-filled tubes of these "Wall o' Water" tepees, which cover and protect young tomato or pepper plants in the spring.

nected end-to-end in long tunnels covering entire rows.

Both kinds of cloches provide protection and allow sunlight to reach the plants. Clear glass cloches also promote warmth because the glass allows the short-wave rays of the sun to enter readily, but the long-wave rays of heat being radiated from the earth cannot so easily escape. Consequently, heat builds up within the cloche.

If you have a way to cut the base off a large wine jug, you'll have your own bell-shaped cloche. Remove its cap during the day to provide ventilation. You can devise other versions of the cloche using plastic milk jugs and soda bottles with their bottoms cut off or large glass jars set upside-down.

Modern plastic equivalents of cloches are available commercially, as are many similar designs. Various plastic domes on the market can be opened at the top for ventilation and stacked together in the garden shed for the winter. Waxed-paper "hot caps" give some protection, though they don't admit as much sunlight. The "solar umbrella" is simply a huge umbrella made of clear plastic that can be set over a plant or several plants. Its handle shaft pushes into the soil to hold it in place, and it collapses easily for storage.

You can also build a portable cold frame—or you can devise a temporary cold frame using hay bales for

Clear glass chloches let sun rays in to warm the soil while retaining the heat that radiates from the earth.

the walls and a storm window for the lid. On especially cold nights, you can raise the temperature in your cold frame somewhat by enclosing several wide, shallow pans of water. As the water freezes, it will release latent heat. Garden writer Nancy Bubel says one pound of water releases 144 Btu's in this way. Just be sure to use shallow pans so the water cools quickly and freezes. Otherwise it won't help much.

If you're going to build a permanent cold frame, consider situating it against the sunny side of your

This makeshift cold frame uses discarded window sashes. But be careful—chips from old lead paint can contaminate your soil.

over this. The manure will soon heat up, but don't plant anything for several days. Wait for the soil temperature to fall and stabilize or the heat will kill your plants.

Some gardeners use an electric heating cable to warm the soil in their hotbeds, but I consider this ridiculously expensive and environmentally *un*friendly. Let's get over such gimmickry, I say.

Cloches and cold frames protect spring seedlings day and night until the weather settles. Other covers—such as inverted flowerpots, paper bags, baskets, and buckets—must be *temporary* nighttime protectors since they exclude sunlight. Occasionally, desperate gardeners set lighted candles under inverted terra cotta pots to provide extra warmth to special plants.

Be sure to secure any lightweight protectors with stakes or rocks or soil. Otherwise, breezes may come up during the night and blow away your covers. For the best insulation, try to cover everything right down to the ground. And to retain the most heat, do your covering well ahead of sunset—before the soil has begun cooling.

Many of these covers will probably work better in the fall, because fall soil is usually warmer than

house or some other heat reservoir. You could even back it up to a basement window, which could be opened to let heat into the frame.

A hotbed is nothing more than a cold frame with its own source of heat. Usually, buried manure provides the heat. Fill a one- or two-foot deep rectangular hole with fresh horse or chicken manure. Water this well to start decomposition, then cover it all with six inches of good topsoil. Place your cold frame

A plastic row cover, stretched over wire hoops or fencing so it doesn't touch the plants, protects cold-hardy greens from fall frosts.

spring soil, as we discussed earlier. Floating row covers are said to provide *three* degrees (Fahrenheit) of frost protection in the spring but *seven* degrees in the fall.

Whatever cover you choose, you'll have to decide when to uncover. Ideally, overnight covers should not be removed until the air temperature has reached 50°F (10°C). Don't be in a rush to whip them off.

The cold air outside the cover can be a shock to tender plants. And plant tissue trying to re-hydrate after a frost responds best to a gradual warming.

It is, however, very important to pay careful attention to plants under glass or clear plastic, because these enclosures can heat up quickly when the sun comes out. If you're not careful, you may save your plants from freezing—only to cook them to death

Cement blocks make an easy-to-build cold frame. The blocks also act as heat reservoirs.

instead. Eliot Coleman, a Maine gardener very experienced with row covers and cold frames, says its better to remove the covers too soon than too late. Put a thermometer in a cold frame, and don't let the temperature inside go much above 60°F or 65°F (16°C or 18°C).

What Doesn't Work

Large commercial growers sometimes employ extraordinary means to save their crops from frost. Giant fans keep the air circulating. Huge foggers envelop whole fields in a moist protective cloud. Obviously, such devices don't make sense for home gardeners, but we may be tempted to try some other extraordinary methods that aren't such good ideas either.

This lettuce is growing under bubble wrap, supported by wire. It's important to open the covers on a sunny day to avoid overheating

Starting a bonfire in the garden may seem like a good way to provide heat, but a bonfire may actually promote cold damage rather than prevent it. The fire tends to send hot air up and away. Meanwhile, the updraft sucks colder air into your garden from surrounding areas. The air circulation may be somewhat helpful, but overall, a bonfire is not worth the effort or the risk.

The same goes for so-called smudge fires, which were sometimes used in fruit orchards. Today they have fallen into disfavor because of the air pollution they create. Besides, the smudge is said to block 90 percent of the radiant heat of the sun yet trap just 20 percent of the earth's heat. So they don't help matters either.

Something else that doesn't work: chemicals. You may have seen advertisements for chemical products that claim to change the freezing point of plant tissue

Aquadomes keep early spring-planted tomatoes from freezing. The wire fencing supports early peas and will later support the growing tomatoes.

earlier, that heat is released when water changes from a liquid state to a solid state (ice). Also, the temperature of water remains at 32°F (0°C) until all of it has solidified. Only then will it drop to match the surrounding air temperature.

Understand, however, that for this to be helpful you must keep spraying *continuously*. That is, your plants must *always* be covered with water that is changing to ice. If you stop spraying, the release of heat also stops, the temperature of the ice falls, and your plants soon freeze. And here's another pitfall: If you keep spraying continuously, the layer of freezing water can become thick enough and heavy enough to break branches or tear off foliage. So my advice is to leave spraying to the professionals.

or to inhibit the formation of ice on crops. Don't believe it. To date, no such product has withstood scientific scrutiny, according to Katharine B. Perry of North Carolina State University.

Similarly, some gardeners may be inclined to try sprinklers in the garden to shower plants with a fine spray of water. Again, commercial growers sometimes do this. It's based on a principle we learned

What about mulch? Does mulching help protect against frost in the kitchen garden? Mulch serves several good purposes. It can help conserve moisture in a dry summer. It can hold down weeds. It can slowly decompose and add organic matter to your topsoil. And, in winter, it can protect hardy perennials by preventing the freeze-thaw cycle that heaves roots up out of the ground.

A traditional fall garden includes vegetables that don't mind frost.

Anything that will hold an insulating layer of warm air around your plants may help extend your harvest into winter.

But I think mulch does not have a clear usefulness in protecting against frost. It's true that, as insulation, it can help the earth retain its heat. But unless you remove the mulch during the day, it will also insulate the earth from the sun's warming rays. The sun warms bare soil more deeply than soil buried under a thick mulch of straw or leaves. Such a mulch might useful for heaping up over plants on a frosty night, perhaps in the strawberry patch, but I hold off mulching in the spring until after the danger of frost has passed.

An exception might be plastic mulch, which can help warm your garden soil. Some gardeners assume that black plastic will warm the soil well because its black color absorbs so much of the sun's heat. Actually, however, the soil is warmed only where it is in contact with the black plastic. A better solution—if you insist on using plastic mulch—is clear plastic. This allows sunrays to pass through but impedes heat from radiating out. It acts like a giant horizontal cloche hugging your row. Clear plastic won't feed your soil or hold back weeds—in fact, it may encourage weed seeds to sprout. But it will help warm your soil deeply, and this warmth may fend off frost on a chilly night.

Some alternatives to plastic have been developed. Black paper mulch has about the same usefulness as black plastic, but it's made from recycled fiber and can be tilled into your garden at the end of the season. Be aware, however, that it contains a chlorine-based antimicrobial chemical not allowed in organic gardens.

I've tested a row cover made from unbleached cotton, similar to cheesecloth in weight and weave. The edges are treated with sunflower oil, which inhibits rotting somewhat. I like the fact that you can compost it when it gets old and raggedy, but it works much better at keeping insects out than at keeping heat in. Nevertheless, I applaud all these efforts to wean us away from petroleum-based gardening, and I look forward to new and better discoveries in the future.

The Aftermath

Let's close this chapter with a few thoughts on what to do when Jack Frost outsmarts you.

If one of your plants wasn't protected adequately and got hit by frost during the night, you might want to try gently spraying it with water the next morning. Do this early, before the sun shines on the plant. Some gardeners have found that this can bring a stricken plant back into the land of the living. The theory is that damage occurs because bright sunlight stimulates metabolic action in the plant while its cells are still dehydrated from the frost. Spraying supposedly helps melt the ice formed in the plant tissues and allows the cells to rehydrate before the plant is stimulated by the sun. Frankly, I've never tried it, but what harm could it do if the alternative is losing a plant?

Once frost has hit, enzymes become active in the affected fruits, causing them to deteriorate rapidly.

If the frost has bitten the actual fruits of your plants—say, the little green peppers or those nice chubby cukes—another question arises. Is it safe to process frostbitten produce for home storage?

The problem is that the frost has started enzymes working in the affected fruit, and this activity causes food to deteriorate rapidly. The result may well be a disagreeable flavor in the processed food, as well as poor color or texture. Nutritionists say the food itself will be safe—with one important exception. *Frosted tomatoes cannot be safely canned.* This is because they no longer have enough acid in them to stay safe during storage after canning. Freezing them as sauce is the safe alternative, but they may not taste so great.

Lastly, once that final killing frost arrives in the fall and lays waste your kitchen garden, clean up the debris. Yes, we're all tempted to leave in the garden those old stalks and blackened plants and that rotten fruit. That's not a bad idea—if you want to provide cozy homes where insects and diseases can spend the winter. The bugs and bacteria will thank you for it.

If you don't feel hospitable toward such things, clean up the mess now. This is especially important for gardeners wanting to wean their gardens from pesticides. Fall cleanup is a nontoxic way to deal with next year's problems.

Of course, some gardeners aren't ready to throw in the trowel quite yet. They have developed ways of gardening *past* frost. We'll meet some of them and explore their methods in the next chapter.

After the final killing frost lays waste to your garden, remove the dead plants. Otherwise, decomposing fruits and plants can provide a hospitable winter habitat for insects and bacteria.

Chapter 6

Gardening Past Frost

Think of it as a northern gardener's dream — a summer that keeps rolling on past the ripening melons, past the dry soup beans, right past the usual fall frost date. I call my dream "August 63rd," because I like to imagine stretching out that warm summer weather for a few more weeks.

The truth is, I doubt I'll ever see August 63rd on any calendar hanging in my garden shed. But I do know of a few northern gardeners who have managed to stretch their gardening season right past frost and into the depths of winter.

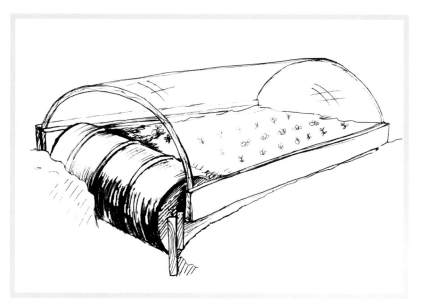

This example of a solar pod incorporates a passive solar collector (barrel painted black) in a sunken base with an insulated plastic cover. The superior insulating value of the cover coupled with a heat reservoir make the solar pod far more effective than a simple traditional cold frame.

Solar Gardening

New Hampshire might seem an unlikely place to find August 63rd, but Leandre and Gretchen Poisson aren't just dreaming about a longer season. With New England determination and Yankee ingenuity, they keep their garden going long after the rest of us have hung up our hoes.

For some thirty years, they've pioneered and refined a style of kitchen gardening they call "American Intensive Gardening." Their aim has been to create a continuous food-producing system that will help gardeners optimize the growing conditions of any climate—including the cold climate of Jack Frost's home turf.

The American Intensive Gardening system relies on age-old organic methods of improving soil fertility and space-age devices for capturing the sun's warmth. These devices include a "solar pod," a reinvention of the cold frame that combines modern insulation with solar engineering.

In their solar pod, the window-sash lid of the traditional cold frame has been replaced by a special curved cover that bulges gently upward. The Poissons construct their special covers using Sunlite, a fiberglass-reinforced plastic sheeting that's lighter and stronger than glass. It's also flexible and easy to work with. The solar pod's cover has a double layer of this Sunlite, with translucent fiberglass insulation sandwiched between the plastic. The upward bulge of the cover captures the sun's rays more efficiently than a flat glass lid. Sunlite's opacity diffuses incoming sunlight yet admits the full spectrum needed by plants.

The eight-by-four-foot solar pod sits atop a sunken base insulated with rigid foamboard. The Poissons say their design provides 300 percent better insulation than a traditional cold frame, extending its usefulness right through a New Hampshire winter. This allows them to grow a dozen or so fresh vegetables all winter long.

Lea and Gretchen have long been committed to feeding themselves as much as possible from their own

This portable cold frame is small, light, and economical.

garden. During summer, they grow the standard fare and preserve much of it. In winter, they feast on this stored produce but enliven their diet with fresh vegetables grown in their solar pods.

To get a continuous harvest, Lea and Gretchen rely on what they call "cool-hardy" vegetables and "cold-tolerant" vegetables. The cool-hardy crops include beets, broccoli, cabbage, lettuce, and others that don't mind cool soil and reduced sunlight. These

crops thrive under the added protection of the solar pods, but the cold-tolerant plants are even tougher. These include turnip greens, collards, kale, leeks, and spinach. While winter rages, they thrive in the mellower microclimates of the solar pods.

Winter isn't the only time the Poissons use solar gardening. To get a jump on spring, they start their plants under huge solar cones made from single layers of Sunlite. Nearly three feet in diameter, these

Wide, raised rows with narrow walkways between them make an efficient use of space, and the loose, raised soil of the beds warms quickly in spring.

cone-shaped devices will later protect many mature plants from fall frosts.

With their solar pods and solar cones, the Poissons have gone beyond my own dream of an August 63rd. As they say in their book *Solar Gardening* (Chelsea Green, 1994), "Our gardening season has neither a beginning nor an end."

Endless Harvest

Meanwhile, over in Maine, Eliot Coleman and Barbara Damrosch have created their own version of an endless gardening season. They have developed a "four-season harvest" that not only puts fresh salads on their table all winter long, but also allows them to run a year-round business supplying salad greens to local restaurants. When I met Eliot and Barbara several years ago, they were well on their way to reinventing the gardening calendar in Maine.

Eliot told how one day he realized that his garden is—believe it or not—at the

Barbara Damrosch and Eliot Coleman harvest year-round in their Maine greenhouse.

Growing inside a greenhouse, such as this unheated greehouse made of plastic sheeting over a frame, will extend your growing season considerably. Many options are available for backyard greenhouses.

same latitude as the sunny south of France. That means he works with the same day length and the same amount of winter sun as do the gardeners in that noted agricultural region of Europe. He and Barbara reasoned that, if they could figure out how to deal with their cold winter temperatures, they would certainly have adequate sunlight for a winter garden.

Their solution has three elements: unheated greenhouses, row covers, and hardy crops. They grow their greens in beds, cover the beds with insulating row covers, and enclose all of this in plastic-covered hoop greenhouses. This double coverage of row cover and greenhouse protects the crops from the extreme cold and the wind. It's basically the same layering technique that we all use when we dress ourselves for cold weather.

Wire wickets hold the row covers about a foot above the soil. The greenhouses are huge tunnel affairs, 30' wide and 100' long.

Their system enables Eliot and Barbara to go inside the greenhouses,

These Jerusalem artichokes could be dug from the soil during winter because they were protected by a thick straw mulch.

uncover the beds, and harvest the greens in relative comfort all winter. Even on cloudy days, the greenhouses are usually warm enough by afternoon to allow them to work in shirtsleeves or down vests. Eliot figures that their system has, in effect, moved his Zone 5 garden to the south by two or three zones.

Barbara and Eliot carefully choose their greens for winter hardiness. Favorites include spinach, tatsoi, Swiss chard, endive, beet leaves, baby carrots, arugula, and kale. Lettuce heads get mushy in the cold, but young lettuce leaves are quite hardy.

Eliot is quick to point out, however, that after the middle of November, most of their greens are hibernating, not growing. In that sense, he and Barbara have extended the harvesting season, not the growing season. Still, some crops, such as mâche, keep growing all winter. Others, such as scallions, can be harvested while frozen, and they will thaw nicely.

Other Ways to Garden Past Frost

If putting up a greenhouse or building a solar pod sounds too complicated to you, then here's a simple way to keep your garden going past frost: bring it indoors. A cook I know always digs up his herbs, transplants them into little pots, and grows them all winter on a window ledge in his kitchen. You can, too.

With a little planning, you can do something similar with larger plants. For example, you can grow peppers or bush tomatoes in a bucket or big pot. Then bring them indoors on nights when frost threatens. Some people grow a whole patio garden in wheeled containers that can easily be pulled to shelter on chilly fall nights.

Plastic domes work well to extend the growing season for cold-resistant plants such as greens.

You can also garden past frost the old-fashioned way. That is, you can grow a traditional fall garden of crops that don't mind frost. Just remember that a fall garden actually has to begin in midsummer, and it won't grow the same way your spring garden did. Since the days get shorter as the season passes, fall crops grow more slowly than those in spring, when each day brings a bit more sunshine than the last. The hardest part is

The hardest part of gardening throughout the winter is learning to time the sowing dates so the crops will be just right for fall and winter harvesting. Eliot explains all about this in his book *Four-Season Harvest* (Chelsea Green, 1992) and in his self-published booklet *The Winter Harvest Manual* (2001).

Brussels sprouts and kale are excellent choices for a fall garden.

knowing when to start each crop. Your best source of help is, once again, more experienced gardeners in your neighborhood.

You can easily fill your fall garden with vegetables that aren't bothered by light frosts. For example, a favorite fall salad green in my household is arugula. The *Selvatica* variety, in particular, holds up through light frosts and loses its sometimes-bitter edge. It goes well with spinach, both in the salad bowl and in the fall garden. Florence fennel grows best in fall and withstands light frosts, and collards love frosty weather. Kohlrabi stays wonderfully crunchy right up until a hard freeze.

Some tender crops have hardier relatives that step

to the fore in the fall garden. Celery can't withstand frequent frosts, but celery root (*celeriac*) will survive even a hard frost if hilled. Onions must be harvested before frost, but scallions can freeze and still recover after thawing.

Most importantly, the fall garden can turn frost from a disadvantage into an advantage because a light frost improves the flavor of many traditional fall crops. Sauerkraut tastes best when made from cabbage that's had a stretch of cool weather and a bit of frost. Brussels sprouts must go through at least two significant frosts to improve their flavor and enrich their vitamin content. Parsnips mature in late fall and sweeten with each frost. Rutabagas are best if left in the ground until hard frosts threaten.

A little frost enhances the flavor of mâche (also known as corn salad or lamb's lettuce). With some protection, this sweet salad plant will keep growing right through winter. French

Leeks can be overwintered and harvested in early spring.

connoisseurs traditionally eat mâche during Lent, since no other fresh greens survive winter so well.

Another advantage of post-frost gardening: no bugs. Or at least fewer bugs. My beds of salad greens always look their best in the fall, after the flea beetles have fled. Even the weeds seem less pesky in the fall.

Unless your weather is severe, many crops can be overwintered for harvest later; a deep mulch may be required in cold climates. Such crops include beets, carrots, parsnips, salsify, scorzonera, and Blue Solaise leeks.

The fall garden also shines a spotlight on some great crops too often overlooked. One of my favorites is kale. Most kale in this country seems to end up decorating the edge of the salad bars in restaurants. Its lush, curly leaves contrast sharply with the pale iceberg lettuce. What an irony. Here in the Northeast, most of that iceberg lettuce was shipped thousands of miles across the country. It's about as tasty and nutritious as a tray of ice cubes—with about the same water content. Meanwhile, next to it lies the neglected kale—easily grown all year in the Northeast, rich in vitamins and iron, and full of flavor. Tell me, why do we serve up the iceberg lettuce and throw away the kale?

At my home, we often eat kale from the kitchen garden all winter long—unless my neighbor's heifers get loose and finish it off before we can. Even when it's frozen stiff you can break off the leaves and bring them inside. Sauté a little garlic in olive oil, chop up the frozen kale a bit, and plop it into the same pan. Cover it, lower the heat, and let it cook just long enough for the kale to burst into a delicious bright green.

Even if you don't get around to growing a fall garden, you can start a garden before winter that will come to life when the snow melts next year. Each fall I start lots of spinach in a cold frame built against the stone foundation of my house. I try to time it so the plants are just emerging when freezing weather sets in. Then I fill the cold frame with fallen tree leaves and forget about it for the winter. When at last the winter weather begins to break, I remove the leaves and close the clear-plastic lid. Soon the soil warms, and

the spinach reawakens from its long slumber. I think there's nothing quite like that first *spring* salad of *fall* spinach.

Jack Frost, eat your heart out.

Embracing Frost

I said at the beginning of this book that we gardeners needn't see Jack Frost as some sort of villain, spoiling our all-too-short gardening seasons. Instead, we can learn to garden *with* frost.

We've now spent quite a few pages learning how to do just that. We've learned how to plan for frost, how to see it coming, and how to fend it off. We've gotten acquainted with our climates and with how frost behaves in our gardens. We've even learned some ways to extend the gardening season right past the frosts of autumn.

But let's not forget another perfectly legitimate way to garden with frost. You can simply content yourself with a shorter gardening season. Hold off planting the spring garden, for example, until the danger of frost has past. Gardening isn't a contest, after all.

So what's the rush? Sure, the early bird gets the worm, but look what the early worm gets.

In the end, this may be the most important thing about frost: *Frost slows us down.* In spring, it tempers our eagerness. In fall, it brings closure and rest. In our gotta-go world—where every nanosecond seems to count—slowness can be a great gift. So rather than see Jack Frost as an adversary, you could choose to greet him as a friend.

When I'm gardening, I try to remember this old French folk saying: *We must go very slowly. We haven't much time.* It reminds me to pay attention, to stay alert, to notice all that I can. The best gardeners I know are the ones who take the time to notice things. After all, a garden can't be rushed. A garden follows its own rhythm. At our best, we gardeners notice and join that rhythm, and that rhythm includes the coming of frost.

I urge you to try this the next time frost arrives in your garden. Ignore

for a while the darkened leaves of the stricken plants. Get down on your hands and knees and look closely at the tiny ice crystals now blanketing your garden. Use a magnifying glass if you've got one handy. You'll find a wonderland in your own backyard.

In its own way, frost may be one of the most beautiful things to happen in your garden all year—as elegant as the loveliest purple eggplant and as delicate as the pinkest pea blossom.

Don't miss it. Like all true beauty, it is fleeting. It will grace your garden for but a short while this morning. To see it, all you have to do is push aside the rush and bustle. Quiet the chatter. For this moment, embrace frost as the beautiful gift that it is.

We must go very slowly. We haven't much time.

Frost Tolerance of Garden Vegetables

Frost damage to crops depends on many factors besides temperature alone. These factors include plant variety, health, and stage of development. Also important are soil conditions, rate of temperature drop, and the length of time the low temperatures persist. Plants may sometimes endure colder temperatures if the cooling comes gradually instead of rapidly.

KEY

✳ Poor; no frost tolerance

✳✳ Good; tolerates light frost

✳✳✳ Great; tolerates hard frost

Vegetable	Rating	Comments
Arugula	✳✳	*Selvatica variety holds up well even in hard frosts.*
Asparagus	✳	*Perennial, but harvest spears before a frost.*
Basil	✳	*Very sensitive to frost.*
Beans	✳	
Beet		
greens	✳✳	
roots	✳✳✳	*Roots may overwinter if mulched.*

Vegetable	Rating	Comments
Broccoli	✳✳	*Young transplants quite hardy. Beyond four-leaf stage, prolonged cold (below 40°F/4°C) may trigger "buttoning."*
Broccoli Raab	✳✳	
Brussels Sprout	✳✳✳	*Needs two significant frosts to improve flavor.*
Cabbage		
seedlings	✳✳✳	*Properly hardened transplants withstand 20°F/-7°C.*
heads	✳✳✳	*Frost improves flavor of heads of some varieties.*
Cabbage, Chinese		
seedlings	✳	*Spring seedlings may bolt in prolonged temperatures below 50°F/10°C.*
heads	✳✳	

117

Vegetable	Rating	Comments
Carrot	✳✳✳	*May overwinter if mulched.*
Cauliflower	✳	*Most finicky of brassicas. Young transplants quite hardy. Beyond four-leaf stage, prolonged cold (below 40°F/4°C) may trigger "buttoning."*
Celeriac		
seedlings	✳	*Spring seedlings may survive a frost, but plants bolt in prolonged temperatures below 50°F/10°C.*
roots	✳✳✳	*Roots may survive hard frosts if hilled or protected.*
Celery		
seedlings	✳	*Seedlings may survive occasional frost, but plants bolt in prolonged temperatures below 50°F (10°C).*
stalks	✳✳	*Inner stalks of mature plants may survive frost.*
Claytonia	✳✳✳	*Extremely hardy; keeps growing if protected.*
Collards	✳✳✳	*Greens taste best after frost.*
Coriander (seeds) or Cilantro (leaves)	✳	
Corn	✳	
Cucumber	✳	
Eggplant	✳	*Drops blossoms in cool weather.*
Endive, Escarole	✳✳	*Protect from hard frosts.*

Vegetable	Rating	Comments
Fava Bean	✳✳	
Fennel, Florence		
seedlings	✳	*Needs cool but frost-free weather to form bulbs.*
bulbs	✳✳✳	*Bulbs may survive hard frosts if hilled or mulched.*
Garlic	✳✳✳	*Plant in fall for harvest the next summer.*
Kale	✳✳✳	*Can freeze solid, recover after thawing.*
Kohlrabi	✳✳	*Early varieties bolt in prolonged temperatures below 40°F (4°C). Bulbs may survive into winter if protected.*
Leek	✳✳✳	*Blue Solaise variety can freeze solid & recover.*
Lettuce		
young leaves	✳✳	*Young lettuce endures frost better in spring than fall. Some leaf varieties survive into winter if protected.*
heads	✳	*Frost turns heads mushy.*
Mâche	✳✳✳	*Extremely hardy; keeps growing if protected.*
Melon	✳	
Mustard	✳✳	*Light frosts improve flavor.*
Okra	✳	*Requires a lot of heat, no frost.*

Vegetable	Rating	Comments
Onion		
bulbs	✳	*Harvest bulbs before frost.*
scallions	✳✳✳	*Scallions can freeze solid, recover after thawing.*
Orach	✳✳	*Thrives in cool weather.*
Parsley	✳✳	*Prolonged cold weather may cause bolting.*
Parsnip	✳✳✳	*Sweetened by frost; overwinter for best flavor.*
Pea		
young plants	✳✳✳	*Young plants may tolerate hard frost.*
flowering plants	✳	*Flowers & pods hurt by frost.*
Pepper	✳	*Drops blossoms in cool weather.*
Potato tubers	✳✳	*Frost may hurt foliage; tubers survive light frost.*
Pumpkin	✳	
Radicchio	✳✳	*Heads may survive into winter if protected.*
Radish	✳✳	*Flavor of fall crop improved by light frost.*
Rhubarb	✳✳✳	*Perennial.*
Rutabaga	✳✳✳	*Needs two significant frosts to improve flavor. Roots may survive into winter if protected.*
Salsify	✳✳✳	*May overwinter if mulched.*
Scorzonera	✳✳✳	*Perennial; hard frost improves flavor.*
Spinach	✳✳	*Overwinter in cold frame for early spring crop.*
Squash	✳	*Both summer & winter squash hurt by frost.*
Swiss Chard		
young plants	✳	*Spring seedlings may bolt in late cold snap.*
mature plants	✳✳	*Hard frost hurts outer leaves of unprotected mature plants, but protected plants may survive into winter.*
Tatsoi		
young plants	✳	*Frost may cause spring seedlings to bolt.*
mature plants	✳✳✳	*Mature plants very hardy if protected.*
Tomato	✳	
Turnip		
greens	✳✳	
roots	✳✳✳	*Roots overwinter if mulched.*

Converting Fahrenheit and Celsius Temperatures

To convert Fahrenheit temperatures to Celsius temperatures, subtract 32 from the Fahrenheit number and multiply the result by 0.556. To convert Celsius temperatures to Fahrenheit, multiply the Celsius number by 1.8 and add 32 to the result.

Celsius and centigrade are practically identical. For quick conversion between Fahrenheit and Celsius temperatures, consult the following chart.

F°	C°	F°	C°	F°	C°	F°	C°	F°	C°	F°	C°	F°	C°	F°	C°
100	38	85	29	70	21	55	13	40	4	25	-4	10	-12	-5	-21
99	37	84	29	69	21	54	12	39	4	24	-4	9	-13	-6	-21
98	37	83	28	68	20	53	12	38	3	23	-5	8	-13	-7	-22
97	36	82	28	67	19	52	11	37	3	22	-6	7	-14	-8	-22
96	36	81	27	66	19	51	11	36	2	21	-6	6	-14	-9	-23
95	35	80	27	65	18	50	10	35	2	20	-7	5	-15	-10	-23
94	34	79	26	64	18	49	9	34	1	19	-7	4	-16	-11	-24
93	34	78	26	63	17	48	9	33	1	18	-8	3	-16	-12	-24
92	33	77	25	62	17	47	8	32	0	17	-8	2	-17	-13	-25
91	33	76	24	61	16	46	8	31	-1	16	-9	1	-17	-14	-26
90	32	75	24	60	16	45	7	30	-1	15	-9	0	-18	-15	-26
89	32	74	23	59	15	44	7	29	-2	14	-10	-1	-18	-16	-27
88	31	73	23	58	14	43	6	28	-2	13	-11	-2	-19	-17	-27
87	31	72	22	57	14	42	6	27	-3	12	-11	-3	-19	-18	-28
86	30	71	22	56	13	41	5	26	-3	11	-12	-4	-20	-19	-28
														-20	-29

Source: James J. Rahn, *Making the Weather Work for You* (Charlotte, VT: Garden Way Publishing, 1979). Reprinted by permission of Storey Books, North Adams, MA.

Resources

Books about Weather

Several of the following books are now out of print (those marked with an asterisk*). But these are often still available in libraries or used-book stores.

David Bowen. *Weather Lore for Gardeners: A Guide to the Accurate Prediction of Local Weather Conditions.** Wellingborough, Northamptonshire, Great Britain: Thorsons Publishers Limited, 1978. A brief (95-page) guide for British gardeners, now somewhat dated. Contains intriguing chapters on "old sayings" and "guidance from plants and animals."

James J. Rahn. *Making the Weather Work for You: A Practical Guide for Gardener and Farmer.** Charlotte, VT: Garden Way Publishing, 1979. A thorough discussion of weather and plant physiology as well as a useful field guide to gardening in general. Includes a chapter on phenology—"nature's own weather instruments."

Calvin Simonds. *The Weather-Wise Gardener.** Emmaus, PA: Rodale Press, 1983. An easy-to-read handbook that covers all aspects of the weather—understanding it, predicting it, and coping with it in the garden. Helpful illustrations. Highly recommended.

Beulah and Harold E. Tannenbaum. *Making and Using Your Own Weather Station.* New York: Venture Books, 1989. A short explanation of how schoolchildren can construct six rudimentary weather instruments to demonstrate the principles of forecasting.

Jane Taylor. *Weather in the Garden.* Sagaponack, NY: Sagapress Inc., 1996. A British gardener's advice on how to help perennials survive winter.

Books about Gardening Past Frost

Eliot Coleman. *Four-Season Harvest.* White River Junction, VT: Chelsea Green Publishing Co., 1992. Coleman's original handbook for extending the harvest of a home garden.

Eliot Coleman. *The Winter Harvest Manual.* 2001. Available from Four Season Farm, 609 Weir Cove Rd., Harborside, ME 04642, or <www.fourseason-farm.com>. Coleman's self-published booklet that spells out how he sells freshly harvested vegetables in Maine from October through May.

Leandre Poisson and Gretchen Vogel Poisson. *Solar Gardening: Growing Vegetables Year-Round the American Intensive Way.* White River Junction, VT:

Chelsea Green Publishing Co., 1994. The Poissons' explanation of their method for using "solar appliances" to stretch the gardening season in New Hampshire. Includes instructions for building these devices.

Internet Websites

For Spacious Skies
www.forspaciousskies.com
An organization dedicated to reminding us of the glorious displays available overhead every day if only we would look up. Sells a beautiful 25"x36" full-color, laminated cloud chart.

Four Season Farm
www.fourseasonfarm.com
Eliot Coleman and Barbara Damrosch introduce their "four-season harvest" system.

Intellicast: Weather for Active Lives
www.intellicast.com
"Dr. Dewpoint" teaches Weather 101 at this website. Also provides frost forecasts, but only on a nationwide basis.

National Weather Service Homepage
www.nws.noaa.gov
Official website of the U.S. National Weather Service. Contains useful data and links to regional Weather Service websites.

University of Michigan's List of Weather Websites
http://yang.sprl.umich.edu/wxnet/
Provides quick access to hundreds of North American weather-related websites.

USA Today Weather
www.usatoday.com/weather/wfront.htm
Colorful graphics and clear language explain weather concepts and make forecasts.

USDA Cooperative State Research, Education, and Extension Service
www.reeusda.gov/
Americans can find their local cooperative extension office with the help of this website.

USDA Plant Hardiness Zone Map
www.usna.usda.gov/Hardzone/ushzmap.html
An interactive map and explanations help Americans determine their garden's hardiness zone.

The Weather Channel
www.weather.com
Web version of the popular television channel.

The Weather Network (Canada)
www.theweathernetwork.com
Forecasts and other weather information for all of Canada.

The Weather Office (Environment Canada)
www.weatheroffice.ec.gc.ca/
Official weather website of the Canadian
government.

Sources for Meteorological Instruments

Davis Instruments
3465 Diablo Ave.
Hayward, CA 94545
(800) 678-3669
www.davisnet.com

Maximum Inc.
30H Samuel Barnet Blvd.
New Bedford, MA 02745
(508) 995-2200
www.maximum-inc.com

Oregon Scientific, Inc.
19861 SW 95th Pl.
Tualatin, OR 97062
www.oregonscientific.com

Wind & Weather
1200 N. Main St.
Fort Bragg, CA 95437-8473
(800) 922-9463
www.windandweather.com

Index

Photo Credits

pages 2, 6, 9, 10, 12, 13 © Walter Chandoha

page 14 © Howard Rice / The Garden Picture Library

page 16 © Mark Turner

page 17 © Walter Chandoha

page 20 © Mayer / Le Scanff / The Garden Picture Library

page 21 © USDA (**Need credit)

page 23, 24 © Walter Chandoha

page 26 © Mark Bolton / The Garden Picture Library

page 28 © Walter Chandoha

page 29 © James Guilliam / The Garden Picture Library

page 30 © Mark Turner

page 33, 34 © Howard Rice / The Garden Picture Library

page 35 © Jerry Pavia

page 36 © Dwight R. Kuhn

page 37 © Jerry Pavia

page 38 © Mayer / Le Scanff / The Garden Picture Library

page 41 © Gary Braasch

page 42 © (left) Walter Chandoha, (center left) Dwight R.
Kuhn, (center right) Walter Chandoha, (right) Mayer / Le
Scanff / The Garden Picture Library

page 43 © Gary Braasch

page 45 © Mayer / Le Scanff / The Garden Picture Library

page 46 © Dwight R. Kuhn

page 48 © Nigel Francis / The Garden Picture Library

page 49 © Dwight R. Kuhn

page 50 © Walter Chandoha

page 52 © Dwight R. Kuhn

page 54, 55 © Mark Turner

page 56 © Walter Chandoha

page 58 © Dwight R. Kuhn

page 59, 60 © Walter Chandoha

page 61 © Jerry Pavia

page 62 © Howard Rice / The Garden Picture Library

page 63 © Walter Chandoha

page 64 © John Ferro Sims / The Garden Picture Library

page 66 © Jacqui Hurst / The Garden Picture Library

page 67 © Walter Chandoha

page 69 © Mark Bolton / The Garden Picture Library

page 70 © Dwight R. Kuhn

page 72 © Walter Chandoha

page 78 © Gary Braasch

page 80 © Paul Rezendes

page 81, 82 © Walter Chandoha

page 85 © Dwight R. Kuhn

page 86, 87, 88, 89, 90, 91, 92, 93, 94, 95, 96, 97 © Walter
Chandoha

page 98 © Gary Braasch

page 99, 100, 103, 104 © Walter Chandoha

page 105 © Barbara Damrosch & Eliot Coleman

page 106 © Gary Braasch

page 107, 108 © Walter Chandoha

page 109 © Jerry Pavia

page 110 © Walter Chandoha

page 111 © Mayer / Le Scanff / The Garden Picture Library

page 112, 113, 114 © Walter Chandoha

page 115 © Gary Braasch

page 116, 120, 122, 126 © Walter Chandoha